LAW–DEATH, GOSPEL–LIFE

Ralph Erskine

Monergism Books

CONTENTS

1. Chapter 1:   1
   The Legal Conviction

2. Chapter 2:   9
   The Doctrine of Justification

3. Chapter 3:   15
   The Believer's Freedom from the Law

4. Chapter 4   23
   What it is to be dead to the law?

5. Chapter 5   31
   The means of death to the law?

6. Chapter 6   38
   The Believer's Life, A Fruit of this Death

7. Chapter 7   54
   The Necessity of this death, in order to this life

8. Chapter 8   71
   Application

9. Chapter 9   82
    Of Examination

10. Chapter 10   93
    Reproof of all Legalists, both doctrinal and practical

11. Chapter 11   107
    Causes of this legal temper

12. Chapter 12   113
    The evil and danger of a legal temper

CHAPTER 1:

The Legal Conviction

"I through the law, am dead to the law, that I might live unto God." Galatians 2:19.

A godly life is what we are all obliged to live, especially if we have been at the Lord's table; but it is a mystery that very few understand in their experience, if they will judge their experiences, by comparing them with this of Paul in our text, "I through the law am dead to the law, that I might live unto God."

Our apostle, in this epistle, is vindicating himself from the base aspersions cast upon him by the false apostles: with respect to his calling, as if he had been no apostle: and with respect to his doctrine, as if it had been false and erroneous. From the beginning of this chapter, to verse 11, he tells us what he hid at Jerusalem; how strenuously he opposed the false brethren, that he might maintain the truth of the gospel, which they sought to overturn. From the 11th verse to the 17th, the apostle tells us what he did at Antioch: how zealously he opposed and reproved

even Peter himself, for his dissimulation, in compelling the Gentiles to
Judaize; giving thereby such offence, that the Jews were confirmed in
their Judaism; "Other Jews dissembled with him, and Barnabas also was
carried away with their dissimulation," (v. 12); and hereby occasion was
given both to Jews and Gentiles, to desert Christ, to deny grace, to return
to the law, and seek justification by the works thereof. So that we may
see here, that great and good men may dissemble, and do much hurt by
their dissimulation, both among ministers and people. We have here a
wonderful example of it in the greatest of men, and such as were pillars
of the church: but it would seem that Peter and Barnabas, and other Jews
here, did not see their fault and sin, but thought they did right enough;
but Paul saw it; "When I saw that they walked not uprightly according
to the truth of the gospel," (v. 14) &c. This might seem a very bold and
imprudent attempt, for Paul, the youngest of all the apostles (I mean,
of whom Christ was last seen, as of one born out of due time) for him
to take upon him to accuse and condemn Peter as well as Barnabas, and
the Jews for their practical error, not walking according to the truth of
the gospel. But we see, that as people may have the gospel, but not the
truth of the gospel; so these that have the truth of the gospel, may be
guilty of not walking according to the truth of it, even as Peter, Barnabas,
and others here, whose dissimulation did not consist with the truth of
the gospel, which they preached, but tended to establish the law, and
so to overturn the gospel. But God hath sometimes very few witnesses
to stand up for the truth of the gospel; here Paul was alone, Peter was
against him, and Barnabas, his own intimate associate, was drawn away
with the dissimulation; Jews and Gentiles were infected, and therefore
Paul alone must fight against them all, for the cause of Christ, and the
doctrine of the gospel, which was endangered, "I said unto Peter before
them all," &c. Not by teaching of any erroneous doctrine did Peter

err, for that is a principle we maintain, that the apostles never erred in teaching, or in their doctrine delivered to the church; but his error was in practice, compelling the Gentiles to Judaize; whereby he gave them occasion to think, that the observation of the law was necessary to justification: whereas he adds, "We that are Jews by nature," &c., (vv. 15,16). We apostles, might he say, though Jews by nature, yet we seek not justification by the works of the law; and therefore, we ought not to drive the Gentiles to the observation of the law, that they may seek righteousness and justification thereby. Why? because,

1. We know that a man cannot be justified by the works of the law, but by the faith of Christ.

2. Because therefore having renounced the law, in point of justification, we have embraced Christ by faith; that through him we may be justified.

3. Because by the deeds of the law, no flesh can be justified.

Now, from verse 17 and downward, the apostle returns to the Galatians; having told how he reproved Peter, and what he said to him concerning justification without the works of the law, he now comes to show this doctrine to be nowise opposite to the doctrine of sanctification, but of absolute necessity to true holiness, (vv.17,18). If we Jews, who lived formerly under the law, and now seek righteousness in Christ alone, are thus accounted as sinners, when we followed the law, it would seem that Christ did disapprove the law, and approve sin: "God forbid," says the apostle; this he denies, and rejects with abhorrence.—To object thus, might he say, against the doctrine of free justification, were egregious blasphemy against the Son of God, as if he were the minister of sin, who came to destroy sin, and to destroy the works of the devil; and by this gospel which I preach, might he say, Christ is held out as the Lamb of God, that taketh away the sins of the world; not to take away righteousness, truly so called, unless it be that false vizard [mask] of legal self-righteousness with which we formerly covered and masked ourselves: nay, he came to bring in everlasting righteousness, a true and perfect righteousness for justification; he came to make an end of sin by the sacrifice of himself, and thereby to purchase the Spirit, as a Spirit of holiness and sanctification, to destroy the power of sin and corruption; and, therefore, it is a base calumny to say that this gospel-doctrine does open the door to sin and licentiousness; this he proves by two arguments,

1. Because the faith of Christ does not destroy itself, "I, through the law, am dead to the law, that I might live unto God," (v. 18). Sin is like an old house which I have razed and destroyed by my doctrine of free justification by faith, and not by works of the law, for by this doctrine I preached freedom from sin through Christ; and, therefore, if I should build up these old wastes of sin again, it is not Christ, but I that would be the sinner, or minister of sin; nay, I would be a madman, to build with one hand what I destroyed with the other.

2. Because liberty to sin is contrary to the very scope of the gospel, and to the design of this doctrine of justification by faith, without the works of the law; "For I, through the law, am dead to the law, that I might live unto God," (v. 19).

This is a very strange and wonderful text, that flesh and blood can hardly hear without suspecting that it savors too much of a new scheme of doctrine; and, if it were not the divinely-inspired words of the apostle, it would hardly escape being taxed as an Antinomian paradox. I remember Luther upon the text says, "The false apostles taught, unless you live to the law, you cannot live to God;" and therefore Paul here must be the most heretical of all heretics; his heresy is unheard-of heresy, reason and human wisdom cannot receive it, that, if we will live to God, we must be dead wholly to the law: yet so it is here, he declares it of himself, and in the name of all believers in Christ, yea, as the very doctrine of faith, "I, through the law, am dead to the law, that I might live unto God."

In which words you may notice two remarkably different things, Death and Life; mortification and vivification. 1. A wonderful DEATH; "I, through the law, am DEAD to the law." 2. A remarkable LIFE, proceeding out of that death: "That I might LIVE unto God."

1st, You have a wonderful DEATH, or Paul's strange mortification; "I, through the law, am DEAD to the law:" and of this mortification we have here three things;

1. The general nature of it, it is called a DEATH, "I am dead."

2. The object of it, The law.

3. The means of it, The law; "I, through the law, am dead to the law;" all very odd things to carnal reason.

1. The general nature of it, it is called a DEATH; "I am DEAD." There are several sorts of death commonly spoken of, viz., temporal, spiritual, and eternal; but this is none of them. Temporal death is a separation betwixt soul and body; but this death takes place where there is no such separation: Paul was thus alive, when he said here, "I am dead." Spiritual death is a separation betwixt God and the soul; but this death is a mean of joining God and the soul together. Eternal death is an eternal separation betwixt God and the soul; but the death here spoken of makes way for eternal communion with God.—This is a strange death, a strange death, a strange mortification: especially if you consider,

2. The object of it, The LAW: "I am dead to the law:" not only the ceremonial law, but even the moral law itself, as under the form of a covenant of works, and as a condition of life. I renounce, might he say, the righteousness of the law, seeking no salvation in the works thereof; nay, in this respect it is dead to me, and I to it; it cannot save me, and I cannot expect salvation by it; nay, "I am dead to the law." To be dead to

sin, is a mortification that people may think they can easily understand; but the mystery of it, in being dead to sin, by this means of being dead to the law, is what cannot be so well understood; for one would think, that to die to the law, were to live in sin: nay, says the apostle, it is quite otherwise; that I die to sin, "I am dead to the law."

3. You have the means of this death, which is strange, namely, The law; "I through the law am dead to the law." As to this mean of death to the law, Viz. THE LAW, I find some divines understand it a different law from the other; as if the apostle should say, "I, by the law of Christ, am freed from the law of Moses; or, I, by the law of faith, am freed from the law of works." But I incline to join with the current of sound divines, who understand both of the same law, q. d., I am dead to the law, THROUGH the law: the law hath taught me that I am a sinner, that cannot be justified by the law, which curses and condemns sinners: "By the law is the knowledge of sin; and having thus by the law known myself to be a guilty wretch, I am dead to all expectation of righteousness by the law. The law then, having thus killed me, and all my hope of life by it, hath been a blest mean of drawing me out of myself, and all my legal righteousness, to seek life and justification in Christ, and his righteousness received by faith. Thus, you have a wonderful death here spoken of.

2dly, You have a remarkable LIFE proceeding out of that death; you may call it Paul's vivification, which was not peculiar to him, but is common to all believers: ""That I might live unto God." Where again you may notice three things. 1. The general nature of this vivification; it is called by the name of Life; while a man is alive to the law, he continues dead; but whenever he is dead to the law, then he is alive; the breath of life is breathed into his nostrils, and he becomes a living soul; for the Spirit of God, the spirit of life enters into him.

2. The object of this life, or vivification, it is God; a living unto God, that is, a new life, a holy life, a divine life; a living to God, to God's honor, to God's glory. Before this, the man lived to himself as his end, as well as for himself as his principle: but now he lives from God as his principle, and to God as his end, which only is a holy life, and wherein true sanctification lies.

3. You have the Influence that this death hath upon this life, or this mortification hath upon this vivification; or, the influence that justification by faith alone, and not by the deeds of the law, hath upon sanctification of heart and life, or living to God, in the particle THAT:

"I am dead to the law, THAT I might live unto God."

Now, might the apostle say, How falsely do you charge my doctrine, as opening a window to licentiousness, while I in the name of all believers declare, that this doctrine of justification by faith alone, or our being dead to the law, in point of justification, does open the door to true holiness: for none can live unto God, till they be dead to the law. "I through the law am dead to the law, that I might live unto God."

But I shall endeavor further to explain the words upon the following observation.

Doctrine: "That to be dead to the law, in the point of justification, is necessary, in order to our living unto God, in point of sanctification: "I, through the law, am dead to the law, that I might live unto God. "Now, upon this doctrine, I shall endeavor, through grace, to explain the several branches of the text; and the general method shall be.

I. To clear and confirm the doctrine.

II. To speak of the believer's DEATH, or mortification, here intended; "I, through the law, am dead to the law."

III. To speak of the believer's LIFE, or vivification; his living unto God.

IV. Of the necessity of this death, in order to this life; or the influence that our being dead to the law hath upon our living unto God.

V. Make some Application of the subject, in sundry Uses.

I. To clear and confirm the doctrine: "At the mouth of two or three witnesses, every word shall be established." But, to show that we are not straitened to find out witnesses to attest the truth of this doctrine, I shall produce more than two or three.

CHAPTER 2:

The Doctrine of Justification

The first witness that I cite, is that where you see, that to be dead to the law, and married to Christ, is necessary, in order to living unto God, bringing forth fruit to him, and serving him in newness of spirit, (Rom. 7:4-6).

The second witness I cite, is very like to this, compared: "Sing, O barren, that did not bear.—For more are the children of the desolate [Gentles] than the children of the married wife," (Isa. 54:1,5). Why? "Thy Maker is thy husband," (v. 5). Being dead to the law, and divorced from it, and married to Christ, the barren woman becomes a fruitful bride. And, lest you think I put a wrong gloss upon this text, and mistake the meaning of it, you may compare it with, A third witness that I cite, whereby this very gloss that I give it, is confirmed, "For it is written, Rejoice thou barren, that bearest not: break forth and cry, that thou travailest not; for the desolate hath many more children than she which hath an husband," (Gal. 4:27).

Now, we would consider what is the subject here spoken of; the apostle is setting forth believers" freedom from the law by the gospel, or their justification by faith, without the works of the law; and he confirms it by an allegory, spewing, that our liberty from the law, was prefigured in the family of Abraham, that we are not children of the bond-woman, or bond-men to the law, but children of the promise, as Isaac: And the apostle explains the prophet, and shows his allegory to be founded, not only on the former historical, but also on this prophetical Scripture. The gospel-church, including all believers among Jews and Gentiles, is called the bride, the Lamb's wife: and as this bride in general, being divorced from the law, and married to Christ, is a fruitful bride, bearing many children, many sons and daughters to Christ, and more under the new dispensation of the covenant of grace, than under the old legal administration thereof before Christ's coming; so every particular believer, being dead to the law, and married to Christ, is, by this means, fruitful in bringing forth the fruits of holiness and righteousness, to the glory of God; as the apostle, in prosecuting this discourse, further shows, "Cast out the bond-woman and her son," (v. 30).

Strange! that the law should be called a bond-woman; and then, "Cast out the bond-woman;" this was strange language; nay, but in the case of justification, "Moses and his tables must give place to Christ," as Luther says. Yea, he adds, in this sense, "I will say to thee, O law, Begone: And if it will not begone, thrust it out by force: Cast out the bond-woman." Further, the apostle adds, "Stand fast, therefore, in the liberty wherewith Christ hath made us free, and be not entangled again with the yoke of bondage," (Gal. 5:1). Read also, verses 4, 5, and 6, where you see, that the believer, being free from the law, and having the spirit of life, and the spirit of faith, bringing forth fruit to God; of which fruits of the Spirit of Christ, in opposition to the fruits of the flesh, you read, verses 16 and 17, and downward. The fourth witness that I cite, is, "You being dead in your sins,—hath he quickened," (Col. 2:13,14). Now, by what means does this quickening, or being made alive to God, come about? It is by the "Blotting out of the hand-writing—nailing to his cross:" Intimating, that there is no living unto God, without being dead to the law, and having the law dead to us, by viewing it crucified with Christ, and nailed to his cross.

The fifth witness is, "For ye are dead, [that is, dead to the law, as he had cleared before, and so dead to sin, self, and the world,] and your life is hid with Christ in God; and when Christ, who is our life, shall appear, then shall ye appear with him in glory. Mortify therefore your members which are upon the earth," (Col. 3:3-5). The believer is said to be dead with Christ, (v. 20), of the preceding chapter, and so dead to the law, which was nailed to the cross of Christ. And, (v. 1), of this chapter, the believer is said to be risen with Christ and so he sits together with Christ in heavenly places: but though his best part is above, even his glorious Head, whom he will follow; yet he hath members on earth, which he is called to mortify; which mortification of sin is, you see, the native fruit of his being dead with Christ, and risen with him.

The sixth witness that I cite, is, "We conclude that a man is justified by faith, without the deeds of the law; and so he is dead to the law," (Rom. 3:28,31). Now, does this doctrine destroy our living to God? Nay, "Do you make void the law, through faith? God forbid! Yes, we establish the law:" We establish it as a covenant of works, while we believe in Christ for righteousness, to be imputed for our justification; and we establish it a rule of life, and holiness, while we believe in Christ for strength, to be imparted for our sanctification; and so being dead to the law, in point of justification, we live unto God in sanctification.

The seventh witness that I cite, is, "Sin shall have no dominion over you; for you are not under the law, but under grace," (Rom. 6:14). Where you see, that a man's being under grace, and not under the law, is the very

means by which he comes to be delivered, and freed from the dominion
of sin, and so lives unto God. Here is the privilege, deliverance from the
dominion of sin; and the means of it is, by the grace of God in Christ
Jesus, by which we are delivered from the law: for, as the motions of
sin, (Rom. 7:5), are said to be by the law, so the law being dead to us,
and we by grace, being married to another husband, we bring forth fruit
unto God; "The grace of God, that bringeth salvation, teaching us to
deny ungodliness," (Titus 2:11). While the law hath power over a man,
he cannot but be bringing forth fruit unto death, (Rom. 7:5).—There
was never yet an effectual course taken for the mortifying of sin, but by
the gospel, and the grace of Christ, which yet some ignorantly think lead
to licentiousness, as they thought in Paul's days, (Rom. 6:15). Nay, while
we are under the law, we are the servants of sin "But now being made free
from sin, and become servants to God, ye have your fruit unto holiness,
and the end everlasting life," (v. 22).

The eighth witness that I cite, is, "For the law of the spirit of life in
Christ Jesus, hath made me free from the law of sin and death," (Rom.
8:2,3). Why? How does that happen? "For what the law could not do,
in that it was weak, through the flesh, God sending his own Son, in
the likeness of sinful flesh; and for sin condemned sin in the flesh," (v.
3). Where you see the quality of every believer; he is one that lives to
God, and walks not after the flesh, but after the Spirit: And now, what
is the foundation of this? Even freedom from the law, which through
our weakness, could not justify us; but our help was laid upon One that
is mighty, who, having come under the law, did, by a sacrifice for sin,
condemn sin in the flesh, that the righteousness of the law might be
fulfilled in us, both in point of justification and sanctification.

The ninth witness that I cite is, "For the love of Christ constrains
us,—that he died for all, that they which live should not henceforth live

to themselves, but to him that died for them," (2 Cor. 5:14,15). There is true sanctification, and living unto God; but how came it about? The means thereof is the death of Christ, which we have been celebrating in the sacrament of the supper; this both the means and the motive thereof. What stronger motive than this, to live to him that died for us; and, by his death, redeemed us from the law? "For we are dead to the law by the body of Christ," (Rom. 7:4); that is, by the death of Christ, the sacrifice of his human nature: and hence comes true spiritual life, or living to him.

The tenth witness that I cite is, "The sting of death is sin, the strength of sin is the law," (1 Cor. 15:56,57). Where the law is called the strength of sin, not only because by the law is the knowledge of sin, and sin would not have power to condemn us, but by virtue of the law, which discharges sin, but also because sin gets strength from the law: "Sin, taking occasion by the commandment, wrought in me all manner of concupiscence; for, without the law, sin was dead," (Rom. 7:8). Sin and corruption are so irritated by the law, that thereby the sinner becomes to be more sinful: which is not the fault of the law, for it prohibits, reproves, and condemns sin: but the fault of corrupt nature, which is so intent in perpetrating evil, that the more anything is forbidden, the more impetuously it follows after it; like a mad horse, the more he is checked with the bridle, the more mad and furious is he. Now, "the strength of sin is the law; but thanks be to God, which gives us the victory, through Jesus Christ our Lord." Victory over the law, which is the strength of sin; and so, being freed from the law, or dead to it, in this way I am freed from sin, and put in case to live unto God.—These are ten witnesses, instead of twenty, that might be adduced for the confirmation of this doctrine, That to be dead to the law in point of justification is necessary, in order to our living unto God in point of sanctification.—Receive this truth, then, in the love of it.

II. The Second thing proposed was, To speak of this strange DEATH of the believer; "I, through the law, am dead to the law." Now, here four things are, to be touched at;

1. What the law is that the believer is dead to?

2. What it is in the law that he is dead to?

3. What it is to be dead to the law?

4. The means of this, that, through the law, he is dead to the law.

CHAPTER 3:

The Believer's Freedom from the Law

1 st, What the law is that the believer is dead to. I know I have need to be cautious what I say in this captious age, especially upon such a subject as this; but it is in the fear of God, to whom I am accountable, and without regard to any man, that I desire to deliver the truths of the gospel.—

What is the law, to which Paul said he was dead? I shall not trouble you with the several acceptations of the law, nor the distinctions of it into judicial, ceremonial, and moral. But here, though the apostle speaks sometimes of the ceremonial, and sometimes of the moral law in this epistle; yet in this text, I suppose, with the current of sound divines, that he understands especially the moral law, or the law of the ten commandments, considered under the form of a covenant of works. The law is to be taken two ways: 1. Materially, for its mere preceptive and directive part.

Or, 2. The law may be taken formally, as it is a covenant, whether of works or grace. Now, the law, materially taken, is still the same, whatever

form it be cast into, and it is the transcript of the divine image, after
which man was created at first: so that, long before the law was written in
tables of stone, it was written in the tables of man's heart; and man was
obliged to give obedience to this law, as a creature to his Creator, though
there never had been any covenant made with him; and this obligation to
obedience is eternal, everlasting, and unchangeable.—But this law was
afterwards cast into two different forms, namely, that of the covenant
of works, and afterwards that of the covenant of grace.—Now, here, I
say, it is meant of the law, or covenant of works; in which law there were
three things, a Precept, a Promise, and a Penalty. 1. The Precept, which
is perfect and personal obedience by our own strength, and in the old
covenant form, Do.

2. The Promise, which is life eternal, Do and Live. 3. The Penalty,
which is death temporal, spiritual, and eternal; if you Do not you shall
Die, (Gen. 2:17). The covenant of works commands good, and forbids
evil, with a promise of life in case of obedience, and a threatening of
death in case of disobedience: and so this law of works hath a twofold
power; a power to justify, and a power to condemn; to justify if we obey,
and to condemn if we disobey. The command of the law, abstractly and
materially considered, is, as I said, eternally binding upon all rational
creatures, so long as they continue to be creatures, and God the Creator;
but the command of the law, formally considered, or under the form of a
covenant of works particularly, binds no longer than the form continues.
Now, the commanding power of the law, as a covenant of works, is a
power calling us to obey (or enjoining us to do) but by our own strength:
to obey, as a condition of life; and to obey, under pain of damnation.

2dly, As to the second thing here, what it is in the law, the believer
is dead to. Here it must be observed, That it is only the believer that is
dead to the law, all others are alive to it; and the believer's being dead

to the law, imports, that he is wholly set free from it; or, as the words of our Confession bear, "They are not under the law, as a covenant of works, to be thereby either justified or condemned." Thus they are dead to the law. The law is compared, in our text, to a hard and cruel master, and we compared to slaves, and bond-men, who as long as they are alive, are under dominion, and at the command of their masters; but when they are dead, they are free from that bondage, and their masters have no more to do with them. Here then, to be dead to the law, is to be free from the dominion and power of the law. Now, I think the power of the law may be considered, either as accidental or essential. It hath an accidental power or strength; for example, by reason of our sinful, corrupt, and depraved state, even an irritating power, whereby, as an occasion, it provokes, and stirs up the corruption of the heart in the unregenerate, (Rom. 7:8). From this the believer is free, so far as he is dead to the law.—But, next, There is a power that the law hath, that may be called essential to it, as a covenant of works: and that is, a justifying and condemning power, as I said before; a power to justify the obedient, and a power to condemn the disobedient: Now, believers are dead to the law, so as they are not under it, to be justified or condemned thereby; they are wholly, and altogether free from the law, as it is a covenant of life and death, upon doing, or not doing.

But, for the further clearing of this, I told you upon that question, what law is here meant? That in the law, as a covenant of works, there are three things.—

1. The precept of obedience.

2. The promise of life.

3. The threatening or penalty of death; all which the believer is dead to.

1. The precept of obedience, as a condition of life, is one part of the covenant of works; "Do and live;" or, "If thou wilt enter into life, keep the commandments:" This the believer is delivered from, and so dead to the precepts of the law as a covenant or condition of life. Take heed to what I say here; I say not, that the believer is delivered from the precept of the law simply, but as a condition of life: for the command of perfect obedience, is not the covenant of works; nay, man was obliged to perfect obedience, and is eternally bound to obey the law, though there had never been a covenant: but the form of the precept, or command in the covenant of works, is perfect obedience as a condition of life.

Now, it is the commanding power of the law, as a covenant of works, that the believer is free from; and it hath no commanding power, but in this strain, namely, to command perfect obedience as the condition of life; and, under pain of the curse, Obey, and thou shalt live; otherwise, thou shalt die. Now, the ground of the believer's freedom from the precept of the law, as a covenant of works, or condition of life, is just Christ's perfect obedience to the law, in his room, in his stead, which is the true and proper condition of our eternal life and happiness: "By the obedience of one, shall many be made righteous:—that as sin hath reigned unto death, even so grace might reign through righteousness, unto eternal life, by Jesus Christ our Lord," (Rom. 5:19-20). There is an eternal truth in this, that life is not to be obtained, unless all be done that the law requires, "Do this and live;" and that is still true, "If thou wilt enter into life, keep the commandments." They must be kept by us, or our Surety: now the Surety's obedience being imputed to the believer, as the condition of eternal-life, the believer is not obliged to obedience to the law as a condition of life; the precept of the law is, Do; but the precept of the law as a covenant of works, is under this conditional form, Do, and Live.

Now, if any say, then the believer is delivered from obligation to do, or to obey the law, I deny that; for this Do, is eternally binding; but the precept of the law, as a covenant of works, is not simply Do, but Do and Live: and this conditional form, which is properly the precept and command of the covenant of works, or as it stood in this conditional Do and Live: for he yielded perfect obedience to it, to procure life by it; and so the believer is wholly delivered from obedience to it; that is, to obtain life by it, or to procure everlasting life by his obedience. The precept, thus formed as the condition of life, by virtue of the annexation of the promise of life to the obedience of it, is the precept of the covenant of works; and from this precept he is freed, and so is dead to the law in respect of the precept of it, in and through Jesus Christ his Surety.

2. The promise of life is another thing in the covenant of works; and this runs in the same line with the former, being so connected with it. The promise of life, in the law, or covenant of works, was just the promise of eternal life, upon condition of perfect obedience: now, the believer's freedom from the law, in this respect, flows from his freedom from it in the former respect: for, if he be freed from the Do, or obedience, as required in that old covenant-form, then he is not to expect eternal life as it is promised in that covenant: nay, the law is divested of its promise of life to the believer: that is to say, his obedience to the law hath not the promise of eternal life, as the legal ground and title upon which he is to obtain it: he holds this title to eternal life in Jesus Christ, his Surety, in whom he hath a perfect obedience, to which eternal life is promised; and which is now the alone sure ground upon which it is to be procured. The believer's own obedience to the law, or his gospel-obedience, and conformity to the law, wrought in him, and done by him, through the help of the Spirit of grace; even this obedience of his, I say, hath not the legal promise of eternal life, as if it were the legal condition of his obtain-

ing eternal life: no, his gospel-obedience hath indeed a gospel-promise, connecting it with eternal life, as it is an evidence of his union to Christ, in whom all the promises are Yea and Amen; and as it is a walking in the way to heaven, without which none shall ever come to the end; "For without holiness it is impossible to see God."—But the legal promise of eternal life made to obedience, and which makes our personal obedience to be the cause and matter of our justification, and as the proper condition of salvation and eternal life, this is the promise of the law, or covenant of works; and this promise it is now wholly divested of, as to the believer in Jesus Christ, who hath taken his law-room, and yielded that perfect obedience, to which the promise of eternal life is now made: and the reason why, I say, the promise of eternal life is how made to Christ's perfect obedience in our room and stead, is, Because, the law, or covenant of works, made no promise of life properly, but to man's own personal obedience; it made no mention of a surety; but now, in sovereign mercy, this law-rigor is abated, and the Surety is accepted, to whose obedience life is promised.

3. The threatening of death, in case of disobedience, is another thing in the covenant of works; death, and wrath, and the curse, is the penalty of the law: death is the reward of sin and disobedience to the law; "In the day thou sinnest thou shalt die;" and this the believer is also freed from by the death of Christ, who died for our sins; the law saith, "Cursed is every one that continueth not in all things written in the book of the law, to do them;" but the gospel saith, "Christ hath redeemed us from the curse of the law, being made a curse for us," (Gal. 3:10-13). As the law then to the believer is divested of its promise of life, so as it cannot justify him for his obedience; so it is divested of its threatening of death, and cannot condemn him for his disobedience to it as a covenant, that covenant-form of it being done away in Christ Jesus, with respect to the

believer. I think some will, perhaps object, saying, That the believer is delivered from the curse of the law, we understand; but still, we cannot fathom how he is dead to the command of the law: that he is dead to the condemning power of the law, is plain; but, how is he dead to the preceptive, mandatory, commanding power of the law? To which it might be replied, He is dead to, and delivered from the preceptive part of the law, not materially, but formally; for the command of it materially, is, Do, or yield obedience: this he can never be delivered from, so long as he is a creature, and God his Creator: but the command of it formally, or under the form of the covenant of works, is, Do, and Live; Do, by our own strength; Do, as the condition of your eternal life; and Do, under the pain of eternal death and damnation: this, I say, which is the commanding part of the law, formally considered, as it is a covenant of works, he is wholly and altogether delivered from. To preach the mandatory part of the law, as a covenant of works, is to preach the moral law, not merely as a rule of life, but as the condition of life eternal; in which sense the believer is not at all bound to acknowledge it: and to say, that the believer is delivered from the law, that is, only from the curse of the law, would make some very strange glosses upon many scriptures: for example, "AS many as are of the works of the law, are under the curse," (Gal. 3:10); the meaning of it then would be, AS many as are under the curse. It must therefore be meant of the precept of the law; As many as are under the precept, are under the penalty thereof. The believer then is to, and delivered from the law in its commanding and condemning power, and that in, and through Christ. And I am not afraid, nor ashamed to say it, in the words of the famous Dr. Owen, "That the whole power and sanction of the first covenant was conferred upon Christ, and in him fulfilled and ended." And I think I say no more than what the apostle, a greater than he, saith, "Christ is the end of the law for righteousness to every one that believeth,"(Rom. 10:4).—Thus you see what it is in the law, the believer died to, more generally.

CHAPTER 4

What it is to be dead to the law?

3rdly, The third thing here proposed was, What it is to be dead to the law, more particularly as it comes under the notion of death. And here, 1. I shall show the Import of this death. 2. Some of the qualities of it.(1.) To show the Import of this death. The notion of death may here help us to the Import; for,

1. As in death there is no relation takes place; it dissolves the relation betwixt master and servant, husband and wife, "The servant is freed from his master," (Job 3:16); so here, the man being dead to the law, the relation betwixt him and it is dissolved, (Rom. 7:1-4). He is now married to Christ and divorced from the law; while the man is alive to the law, the relation stands; "For I testify to everyone that is uncircumcised, that he is a debtor to do the whole law," (Gal. 5:3).

2. In death there is no care or thoughtfulness, (Eccl. 9:10), "There is no work, nor device, nor knowledge, nor wisdom in the grave, whither thou goest;" intimating to us that in death there is no care nor thoughtfulness, nor concern about doing anything; so the man that is dead to the law, he hath no more care nor concern about the works of the law, in point of

JUSTIFICATION, than a dead corpse about the work in which it was occupied whilst living: while the man is alive to the law, all his care and concern is about the works of the law; "Do and Live."

3. In death there is no hope; "The land of the living is the land of hope," (Eccl. 9:4): even so the man that is dead to the law hath no hope nor expectation from the law, or from his obedience thereto.—The man that is alive to the law, he hath hope that God will pardon him, and pity him: why? because he does so and so: he is a good neighbor, he wrongs nobody, he is just in his dealings, and careful in his duties; and, touching the righteousness of the law, he is blameless; he hath a good heart toward God, and he hath a good life too; and therefore he, hopes to be justified and saved of God, for Christ's sake: for he hath learned, it may be, to make so much use of Christ, as to think he cannot be saved without him, but still his hope and expectation is founded upon the law. But now, the man dead to the law, he hath no hope from the law; nay, he despairs of salvation by the deeds of the law; as he sees he cannot do anything without grace and strength from above, so even, when he does anything by the help of grace, he sees it so lame and imperfect that God cannot justify or save him, to the honor and credit of his justice, unless he hath a perfect righteousness. He hath no hope by the law.

4. In death there is no toil, no turbulent passion or affection: natural death puts an end to natural affections, which take place in man's lifetime; such as the weary pursuit of what we love, and the wearisome flight from what we hate, or fear; there is no such thing in the grave; "There the weary are at rest," (Job 3:19). They that are alive to the law, and find the life of their hands, they weary themselves in the greatness of their way, as it is expressed, (Isa. 57:10).—Many a weary night and day they may have in pursuing after their lovers, in establishing their darling self-righteousness. The law gives them a wearisome task, to make brick

without affording straw; and loads them with heavy burdens of curses, in case the task be not performed.—But, when a man is dead to the law, then the weary are at rest: Christ is the rest; "Come to me, all ye that are weary and heavy laden, and I will give you rest." Then the man gets rest to his conscience in the blood and righteousness of Christ, the end of the law; rest to his passions and affections; he rests from his fears, legal fears of hell, and wrath threatened in the law; the believer indeed may be filled with them, but so far as he is dead to the law, so far is he at rest from these legal slavish fears. He rests from his love and delight; the law affords its votaries much pleasure, sometimes in the performance of their duty in a legal way; but now the believer takes no delight in that way of justification; he is out of conceit with himself and his duties, because they are vile; yea, though they were not so vile as they are, but perfect, yet he is out of conceit with that way of life; and beholding the glory of the new covenant and way of salvation, joins issue with Job, "Whom, though I were righteous, yet would I not answer, but I would make supplication to my judge; though I were perfect, yet would I not know my soul, I would despise my life," (Job 9:15-21). In a word, he rests from his legal grief and sorrows because he rests from his legal labors. As it is said of the dead in Christ, in another sense, "Blessed are the dead that die in the Lord, they rest from their labours, and their works follow them," (Rev. 14:13): so I may say in this case, Blessed are the dead that die to the law, they rest from their labors, their toilsome, troublesome, wearisome, legal works, and yet their works do follow them; they are now created in Christ Jesus unto good works. But,

5. In death there is no sense: a dead man does not see, nor hear, nor taste, nor smell, nor exert any natural sense; so that they are dead to it, they do not now see the lightnings of Sinai all in a flame, as formerly they did; they do not hear the thunders thereof; they do not smell the

sulfur of the burning mountain, they do not feel the terror of vindictive vengeance, the tempest that surrounded the mount, they do not taste the gall, the bitterness of the wrath threatened in the law; the bitterness of death is over with them, so far as they see that Christ drank the gall for them; yea, so far as they are dead to the law, they are dead to all Sinai wrath: "They are not come to the mount that might not be touched, and that burned with fire, nor unto blackness, and darkness, and tempest, and the sound of the trumpet, and the voice of words, but they are come to mount Sion, and unto the city of the living God," (Heb. 12:18-24). But what? Have the godly no sense of law-wrath? Yea, so far as they are legal, and under the law (for they are never wholly freed from a legal temper while here) the dead ghost of the law may rise up and fright them; but, so far as they are dead to the law, it is not law-wrath, but fatherly wrath that affects them. Indeed, through unbelief, they may fear hell: but they cannot do so by faith, seeing there is no foundation for either that faith or fear in the Bible, that a believer shall be cast into hell, since there is no condemnation to them that are in Christ Jesus.

6. In death there is no motion; vital motion ceases when death takes place: thus, so far as a man is dead to the law, so far, the motions of sin are killed; for, "The motions of sin are by the law," (Rom. 7:5). By the law occasionally and accidentally men running the more into sin, by how much the more they are forbidden to commit sin. Hence Musculus compares the law, in this respect, to a chaste matron in a brothel-house; which, by her good advice, does prove an occasion to some impudent whores to be more bold and impudent in their impiety; "Sin, taking occasion by the law (or commandment, saith the apostle), wrought in me all manner of concupiscence." But now, so far as a man is dead to the law, so far are the motions of sin killed, and his soul quickened to live unto God; of which more afterwards.

(2.) To show some of the qualities of this death to the law.

1. It is an universal death; I do not mean that it is common to all the children of men; though it be a common death to the children of God, and to every one of them, yet it is a rare death among the children of men; "The whole world lies in wickedness, and are dead in sins and trespasses:" few are dead in this sense; but, what I mean by its being universal is, that the man is dead to the law in point of justification, he is dead to every part of the law in its old-covenant form, to the precept of it, to the penalty of it, so as he is not to be justified by the one, nor condemned by the other. He is dead to every legal form of the law; his gospel-obedience thereto is no part of his righteousness for justification before God, if he should endeavor to make his gospel-obedience to the law as a rule of life in the hand of a Mediator, any part of his righteousness for justification, he so far turns the covenant of grace, and the duties required therein, into a covenant of works, and he seeks to live unto that to which he is, and should be dead. It is true, the form of the law in the gospel-covenant does not require obedience for justification, but yet this corrupt nature is prone to turn to the old bias, and abuse the proper form of it, by turning of the rule of obedience into a rule of acceptance.—If a man make faith itself an act, or any act or fruit of it the matter of his justification, he turns it to a covenant of works; the believer is dead to faith itself in this respect: yea, faith renounces itself and all things else, but the righteousness of Christ, for justification. In this sense he is dead to repentance, love, and other graces; he is dead to every obedience to the law, as a covenant of works; to his natural legal obedience before his conversion, and to his spiritual gospel-obedience after conversion; which, though it be a righteousness that God works, and is the Author of it, yet, because it is the believer that is the subject, and made the actor thereof, it is called his own righteousness, or conformity to the law; all

which he renounced in the matter of justification, desiring to be found in Christ, not having his own righteousness, that is after the law, but the righteousness which is of God by faith, (Phil. 3:9). So that I say, it is a universal death.

2. It is a lingering death. It is not easy to get the law killed; something of a legal disposition remains even in the believer while he is in this world: many a stroke does self and self-righteousness get, but still it revives again. If he were wholly dead to the law, he would be wholly dead to sin; but so far as the law lives, so far sin lives. They that think they know the gospel well enough bewray their ignorance; no man can be too evangelical; it will take all his life-time to get a legal temper destroyed. Though the believer be delivered wholly from the law, in its commanding and condemning power and authority, or its rightful power that it hath over all that are under it: yet he is not delivered wholly from its usurped power, which takes place many times upon him, while here, through remaining unbelief.

3. It is a painful death; it is like the cutting off the right hand and plucking out the right eye: The man hath no inclination to part with the law. It is as natural for him to expect God's favor upon his doing so and so, and to expect life and salvation by his own obedience, or doing as well as he can, as it is natural for him to draw his breath: If we do our best, God will accept of us! That is the natural language of everyone who is wedded to the Do and Live of the first covenant. And O what a pain is it to be brought off from that way! To die to the law, is most unnatural, strange doctrine: and legal pangs, and pains of conviction, and humiliation must be borne, before a right thought about dying to the law can be brought forth.

4. It is a pleasant death; it is painful at first, but pleasant at last: O how pleasant is it, to see self-abased, and grace exalted; self-righteousness cried

down, and Christ's righteousness cried up in the soul! "Wisdom's ways are pleasantness:" and this way, particularly, wherein no flesh does glory in his presence; but he that glorieth, glorieth in the Lord: he rejoiceth in Christ Jesus, and hath no confidence in the flesh: he doth joy in God, through Jesus Christ, by whom he receives the atonement; and grace requiring, through righteousness, to eternal life, by Jesus Christ, our Lord, (Rom. 5:11,21). This death is a pleasant parting, when the man is brought to a parting with all his own rags for a glorious robe, (Isa. 64:6; 61:12; 45:24).

5. It is an honorable death: to be dead to the law is a death that brings honor to God, to Christ, to the law, and to the believer. It brings honor to God's holiness, which is now satisfied by Christ's doing; and honor to God's justice, which is now satisfied by Christ's dying.—It brings honor to Christ; for now the man values the righteousness of Christ, as being indeed the righteousness of God, and a full, sufficient, perfect righteousness.—It brings honor to the law, when, instead of our imperfect obedience, we bring to it an obedience better than men or angels in their best estate could give it, even the Law-giver's obedience; which indeed doth magnify the law, and make it honorable.—It brings honor also to the believer himself: he is honored and beautified with a law-abiding righteousness, truly meritorious, and every way glorious: "This is the honor of all the saints."

6. It is a profitable death: it is a happy death: and a holy death: profitable both for happiness and holiness; profitable both for justification and sanctification. Our legal righteousness is unprofitable: "I will declare thy righteousness, and thy works; for they shall not profit thee," (Isa. 57:12). It is unprofitable for justification; for, "By the deeds of the law, shall no flesh be justified." It is unprofitable for sanctification; for his filthy rags do rather pollute him than purify him.—But the righteousness

of Christ is profitable every way: they are happy that have it; for, they are justified from all things, from which they could not be justified by the law of Moses: they are holy that have it; as will appear in the sequel of our discourse. Being dead to the law, is the way to live unto God.

CHAPTER 5

The means of death to the law?

4thly, The Fourth thing here proposed, is the means of this death; "I, THROUGH THE LAW, am dead to the law:" the means of death to the law, is the law. But then a question may be removed, how can this be, seeing the law is the cause of no good thing in use and is the ministration of death and condemnation? (2 Cor. 3:7-9). — In answer to which, we may observe, That though the law is not the cause of this death to the law, and so death to sin; yet it is an occasion thereof, for it accuses, terrifies, and condemns us, and therefore occasions and urges us to flee to Christ, who is the true cause that we die to the law, and to sin: as the needle goes before, and draws the thread which sews the cloth, so the needle of the law goes before, and makes way for the grace of the gospel, that it may follow after, and take place in the heart. To be dead to the law, and married to Christ, is all one in Scripture-sense. Now, to be DEAD to the law, is by means of the law, to be led to Christ for justification, by faith in him, without the deeds of the law; "The law was our schoolmaster to lead us to Christ, that we might be justified by faith," (Gal. 3:25); where the law may be taken either for the ceremonial or moral law. If we take it for the ceremonial law, then it is true that the ceremonial law pointed out Christ to us truly: but then the ceremonial law was gospel, in the substance of it, though veiled over with types and shadows, which were to continue till the body was come: but if we take it for the moral law, then it brings us to Christ only occasionally; for to bring us to Christ, is no proper work of the law, only it is the occasion thereof, insomuch as it forces us from itself; and makes us to see that by it there is no hope of life; so it curses all sinners, and gives hope of life to none: it is the gospel only that shows us the salvation to be had in Christ. Now, the law, by the severity of it, is an occasion to us of seeking life, where it is to be found: like a child, knowing the tenderness of his father's love, and finding the school-master to be very severe and sharp, he runs from the severity, of the master, to hide himself under his father's wings: yet not by his master's teaching, but his severity is the occasion of it: even so it is through the law, and its severity, that the believer is dead to the law: it is then by a law-work, in some measure, a work of legal conviction and humiliation, that a man comes to be dead to the law.

Here I will name to you a few pieces of law-work, which are the occasion of the man's being dead to the law, when the Spirit of God makes use of the law for that end.

1. Through the law, a man gets the conviction of the holiness of God, and of the holiness, spirituality, and extent of the law itself; the Spirit of God enlightens the mind, to see the conformity of the command unto the will of God, and to the holy nature of God; this is called, The coming of the commandment, "For I was alive without the law once," (Rom. 7:9): I thought I was holy enough; I found the life of my hand, while I was, "Touching the righteousness of the law, blameless: But when the commandment came, sin revived, and I died." When I saw the holiness and spirituality of God's law, sin revived, and I died; I saw that I was

a sinner indeed, and I died to the law, and to all conceit of my own works, and obedience to the law. This conviction makes a man have a doctrinal approbation of the law as holy, just, and good: holy in its precepts: just, in its threatenings; and good in its promises; I consent to the law, that it is good. By this conviction, a man sees not only the holiness and spirituality, but the extent of the law;

"Thy commandment is exceeding broad;" it is extended to all my thoughts, words, and actions; to all my affections, designs, desires, and inclinations. Now, when a man sees this, it kills his confidence, and makes him see he hath no righteousness conformable to the law.

2. Through the law, the man gets the conviction of sin; "By the law is the knowledge of sin," (Rom. 3:20). Conviction of sin is the consciousness of our transgressing of this holy law. This conviction makes a man see sin in its nature, that it is the transgression of the law, (1 John 3:4), and so a contrariety to the whole nature and will of God. This conviction makes a man see the kinds of sin: it may be, the Spirit of God begins with some actual grievous sin: actual sin is the swerving of our actions, either in thought, word, or deed, from the law of God, either by omission or commission. From thence the conviction goes to original sin, letting the man see, that not only is his nature destitute of all righteousness, and conformity to the law, but that it is wholly corrupt, that he is just a hell of sin and enmity against God: and from thence the Spirit of God by the law, convinces the man of the originating sin, even of Adam's sin, and says to him, as it is, "Thy first father hath sinned," (Isa. 43:27), and thou in him.—This conviction makes a man to see also the aggravations of sin, how much light, and how many mercies he hath sinned against: And also the power and dominion of sin, what a slave he is thereto, and that the law is so far from freeing him therefrom, that it but exasperates corruption, and so is the strength of sin: Now when the man comes thus

to see sin in its nature, kinds, aggravations, and dominion, what can more tend to kill his conceit of righteousness by the law?

3. Through the law the man gets the conviction of guilt as well as sin, that he is bound over to punishment according to the law: for guilt is properly an obligation to punishment. As by the precept of the law, the man comes to get the knowledge of the intrinsical evil of sin in its nature; so by the penalty of the law, he comes to get the knowledge of the consequential evil of sin, as binding him over to hell, death, and damnation; that the curse of God, the wrath of God, the vengeance of God is the retinue and train of attendants that accompany sin: and so the man is put in fear of hell and damnation. It may be, when he goes to bed, he shall never rise again; when he goes out, he thinks he shall never come in again; he is afraid his meat choke him, or the house fall above his head, or the earth open and swallow him up: sense of wrath haunts him like a ghost; the man is put in prison, and concluded under sin, (Gal. 3:22). Sin is the prison, the sinner is the prisoner, God is the Judge, and the curse of the law is the bond by which the prisoner is tied neck and heel; and from this prison there is no escape, without the mercy of God in Christ.

Who can command this prisoner to come forth? The law cannot do it; it is weak through the flesh: man cannot do it, he is by nature without strength: only He, whom God hath given to be a covenant to the people, can say to the prisoner, "Go forth," (Isa. 49:6-9). Now, when the man is thus convinced of guilt and wrath by the law, this hath a tendency to make him dead to the law, and to kill his confidence in any legal righteousness of his own. O! is there any poor prisoner here, that finds himself shut up in prison, under the power of sin, and under the guilt of sin, and wrath of God? O let this give you some comfort for the present, till God loose your bands, that this is the way God is taking to make you dead to the law, that you may live to God.

4. Through the law, a man gets the conviction of God's equity and righteousness, though he should punish and execute law-vengeance; and so he is made to justify God, though he should send him to hell. I do not say, that the sinner is made content to be damned; no: that, in some respect, were to be content to be an enemy to God, and to sin against him forever; for, the state of the damned includes everlasting enmity and sin, and so it can never be the thing he is made content with; but the man is brought to a conviction of God's equity and righteousness, though he should send him to hell, as an everlasting punishment. "To justify God," says an eminent divine, "is to acknowledge on the one hand, that he does no wrong to the sinner in the execution of the curse; and, on the other hand, that he does no wrong to himself, or to his own justice, when he executes the judgment threatened against sin, but that he does that which is right." O, says the sinner, in this case, God does me no wrong, though he should destroy me; and he does not wrong his own justice, but is a just God in so doing; yea, I cannot see how the credit of his justice should be salved, and how he should be glorified in his justice, if he do not execute judgment upon me, either in myself, or in a surety for me, because I have offended such an infinitely glorious Being: "Against thee, thee only have I sinned—that thou mightest be justified when thou speakest; and clear when thou judgest," (Ps. 51:4). Is God unrighteous, that takes vengeance? God forbid," (Rom. 3:5,6). The offence done against the greatest of Beings, deserves the greatest of punishments, even the eternal destruction of the creature. It is true, God delights not in the death of a sinner; "As I live, I have no pleasure in the death of a sinner," (Ezek. 18:32); that is, as it is a destruction of the creature, though he delights in it, as it is the execution of justice: even so,

the sinner convinced by the law, though he cannot take pleasure in this, to think of being destroyed, yet there is some secret kind of justifying that which God takes pleasure in, namely, the execution of justice. O how fit is it, that God's justice be glorified! And how just is God, in executing infinite judgment upon such an infinite evil as sin is! And indeed the sinner would not see salvation to be free, if he did not see damnation to be just; but the sight of this, in the glass of the law, and in the light of the Spirit, tends, in a manner, to reconcile the man with the device of Salvation through Christ, whose bloody sacrifice gives justice full satisfaction.—

He is now content that God's justice be glorified by a satisfaction more glorious than that which the damned in hell can give; and so it tends to make him dead to the law, and to all other legal penances, and sham satisfactions, which those, who are ignorant of God's equity and righteousness, are ready foolishly to invent.

5. Through the law a man gets the conviction of his own inexcusableness, which is that effect of a legal work of the Spirit, whereby the soul is left without excuse of, or defense for itself:

"Whatsoever things the law saith, it saith to them that are under it, that every mouth may be stopped, and all the world may become guilty before God," (Rom. 3:19).

Now the whole soul of man cries out, Guilty, guilty; his fig-leaves of excuses are blown away; his former shifts and cavils, in defense of himself, do now vanish: he hath not a word to speak in favor of himself.

What said he formerly? Why, it maybe, his heart said, if not his mouth, O I hope there will be no fear of me, Adam's sin was not mine; original sin is what I could not help, it came with me to the world; as for my actual sins, I see others guilty of greater; as for my omission of duties, and commission of trespasses, I see none but have their faults; and God is a merciful God, and I hope he will not be so unjust as to damn his own creatures.—These, and the like, shifts and excuses, formerly took place; but now he becomes speechless; his mouth is stopped. They see they will but deceive themselves, by these miserable shifts; and that they are guilty, guilty, and sinful wretches, blacker than the very devil, and have not a mouth to open for themselves; and so they die to all conceit of themselves, and their own righteousness.

6. Through the law the man comes thus to get a conviction of his absolute need of the gospel, or of the SAVIOUR revealed thereby; being convinced of his sinful and miserable state by nature, and humbled under the serious consideration and view of his sin and misery, fearing the wrath of God due to him for sin, beholding the equity of God, though he should cast him into hell; having his mouth stopped, and despairing of getting out of this condition, by his own power, or the help of any other creature; he is now convinced of the need of a Saviour: O I perish, I perish forever, unless the Lawgiver provide a law-binding righteousness for me! Now, the soul is ready to cry out, not in Rachel's sense, "Give me children, or else I die;" but in her phrase, O give me Christ, or else I die; give me a Surety, or else I die. Now, he is content to be forever indebted to the righteousness of another: and thus the law is the occasion of bringing a man to Christ. And so you see how it is, that through the law, they are dead to the law, that they may live unto God.

CHAPTER 6

The Believer's Life, A Fruit of this Death

The Third thing is to speak of the believer's LIFE, which is the fruit of this death; it is a living unto God. And now, in speaking hereto, I would,

1. Inquire what kind of life it is?

2. What are the scriptural designations of it?

3. What is imported in its being called a living in general?

4. What is imported in its being called a living unto God in particular?

1st, What kind of life is it that the believer hath in consequence of his being dead to the law?

And, 1. It is not a natural life, either in a physical or moral sense. Natural life, in a physical sense, is that which we received from Adam by generation; and it is the function of natural faculties, in living, moving, using of sense and reason; that is a life that is common to all men, who yet may be dead; neither is it a natural life in a moral sense, such as heathens may have; the heathens may have common notions of God, and of good and evil, so as to render them inexcusable in their unnatural immoralities, (Rom. 1:19,20). They have a book of nature, both internal, in the remainders of the law in their heart, so as they do by nature the things contained in the law, (Rom.2:14,15), and external, in God's works of creation and general providence; "The heavens declare the glory of the Lord, and the firmament sheweth his handy-work," (Ps. 19:1). Now, this natural life cannot be the living to God here spoken of, because this natural life flows only from a natural state, which is a state of death: by nature we are dead, legally dead under condemnation; spiritually dead in sins, wholly corrupt, and the tree being bad, the fruit must be bad also: a filthy fountain can bring forth nothing but filthy streams.—This natural life does proceed from natural principles, and these are corrupt; such as the desires of the flesh and of the mind; the lusts of the flesh, the lust of the eye, and the pride of life. At best their natural life flows from self-love, or love to its own honor, praises, profits, or pleasures: all nature's works are selfish, however heroic they may be. This natural life is directed by a natural rule, such as the light of nature inwards, or outward, accompanied with the counsels and examples of naturalists; neither does it ever come up to that same rule of nature's light, which therefore does condemn them as guilty. This natural life hath only natural designs, and ends: the natural man acts from self as his principle, to self as his end, ascribing the glory of all his actions thereunto: thus Herod gave not God the glory of his fine oration, but took the praise to himself; but he was immediately smitten of an angel, and eaten up of worms.—This natural way of living, it is in a natural manner, after the course of this world, according to the prince of the power of the air, (Eph. 2:2), which is nothing but a walking in the lusts of the flesh, fulfilling the desires of the flesh and of the mind: yea, in this natural life, nothing of Christ, or of his gospel, is either in the state, practice, rule, end, or manner of it; nay, they are without Christ, being aliens from the commonwealth of Israel, and strangers to the covenant of promise; having no hope, and without God, [or ATHEISTS] in the world, (Eph. 2:12).

2. It is not a legal life, either of Jewish conformity, to the ceremonial law, or of perfect conformity to the moral law: It is not that legal life of Jewish conformity to the ceremonial law, or according to the Old Testament dispensation; for that ceremonial law is abrogated in Christ, the substance of all the old shadows; and so that Jewish life is unprofitable, and vain; yea, it is damnable, and prohibited under the highest penalties, (Col. 3:20,21). And therefore, says the Apostle, "If ye be circumcised, [or live according to the ceremonial law, or any other law of works, so as to expect justification thereby,] Christ shall profit you nothing," (Gal. 5:2). Neither is this living to God that perfect life of conformity to the moral law, according to the old covenant of works, which required perfect, personal, and perpetual obedience, as the condition of life; and threatened death upon the least failure: I say, it is not this life either: for man hath become guilty, and forfeited life, and incurred death by Adam's first transgression; "By one man sin entered into the world, and death by sin; and so death passed upon all men, for that all have sinned," (Rom. 5:12). Thus we are forever incapable of that life, which Adam was capable of before the fall. It is also impracticable, because man is by nature without strength, (Rom. 5:6).

We have no strength to give that obedience which the covenant of works requires, because we must be redeemed from the curse thereof, and restored to the righteousness thereof, before we can be capable to do what it requires.—And though Adam's sin and transgression were not imputed to us, as indeed it undoubtedly is, yet seeing every adult person at least hath sinned after the similitude of Adam's transgression; for, "No man liveth and sinneth not;" therefore he can never perform the perfect obedience therein required; and, "By the deeds of the law, no flesh can be justified." Besides, there is no article of the covenant of works, that provided for a remedy in case of a breach; but all that the covenant of works doth, is, to promise life to perfect obedience in man's own strength, and threatens death in case of failure, and so leaves the transgressor thereof under its curse.—In a word, the life according to that covenant cannot be the life here meant, because that covenant speaks nothing of Christ, or of his gospel, by whom, and by which, only we can now come to this living unto God; and because this living unto God presupposes a being dead to the law, or dead to that covenant, otherwise we can never live unto God.

3. It is not a Pharisaical life of external, legal, but imperfect conformity to the law, and thereby endeavoring to establish a righteousness of their own, as the Jews, (Rom. 9:31,32; 10:3). Many reckon an outward moral conversation to be this living unto God, whether in performing the natural duties of civility and moral honesty, or in an external performance of religious duties, such as prayer, praise, reading, hearing, and waiting upon divine worship. The church of Laodicea was self-conceited; they thought they were rich, and increased with goods; but, behold the testificate that Christ gave them, that they were neither cold nor hot, such as God would spew out of his mouth, yea, that they were wretched, miserable, blind, and naked; that is all the testimony that he gave them, who looked upon themselves as rich in legal righteousness, and good works. This Pharisaical life may be accompanied with a glorious profession; they may profess soundness in the faith, and disown all these legal and unsound principles which others may have as their stated opinion: they may profess that righteousness and justification is not by the works of the law, but by the faith of Christ, or by the works of Christ received by faith alone; they may have a sound head, but no sound heart, nor a good conscience, nor faith unfeigned, for the end of the commandment

is love, proceeding from these, (1 Tim. 1:5). People may be like the toad, that hath a precious stone in his head, but hath his belly full of poison; they may have a head full of knowledge, and a heart full of enmity; a filthy mud wall may be garnished with fine arras; a rotten sepulchre may be whitened: they may have much of the matter and external form of godliness, and yet want the power and internal form thereof, a name to live, and be dead. Yea, this Pharisaical life may be accompanied with many excellent gifts, and common graces, and high attainments (as well as all visible church privileges), as we find some apostates may have, (Heb. 6:4-6). Their understanding may be so far enlightened that they may attain to strange discoveries of Christ. Balaam was called a man whose eyes were opened, and that saw the visions of the Almighty, (Num. 24:2,3,4,15). Their wills maybe so far renewed as to have a great many good purposes, like these who resolved to serve the Lord with all their heart, (Deut. 5:27-29; Josh. 24:18-21). They may be almost persuaded to be Christians; their affections may be greatly raised and enlarged; they may be raised to some sorrow for sin, like Judas, and like Esau, who sought the blessing with tears; to some joy, like the stony-ground hearers, who received the word with joy and pleasure, yet had no root; to some delight, like the Jews, of whom it is said, (Isa. 58:2), that they sought him daily , and delighted to know his ways; yea, to some fear and reverence, like these enemies that are said to submit themselves, (Ps. 66:3), and even to some extraordinary raptures, like these who are said to taste of the heavenly gift, and to be partakers of the Holy Ghost. On all which accounts their life and conversation may be changed in part. Thus many, "through the knowledge of God and of Christ, have escaped the pollutions of the world," (2 Pet. 2:20-22). The common gifts and graces of the Spirit may warm, smooth, and wash their outward conversation;

all this will not amount to this living unto God in the text. Well, what kind of life is this? We reply,

4. It is a spiritual life, being the action, motion, and gracious saving operation of the Spirit of God in us, causing us to walk in his statutes, (Ezek. 36:27), it is the life of a spiritual man. It is impossible for one to have a godly life, whatever to the world he may seem to have, till he be a godly person, or in a spiritual state. A man must have a state of union to Christ by the faith of God's operation, so that, being married with his Husband, he may bring forth fruit unto God. The branch of the old Adam cannot bear good fruit; it is only the true branch, planted in Christ by the spirit of faith that bears good fruit, (John 15:4,5). A man must be in a state of reconciliation with God, justified, pardoned, and indemnified before God accept of any service off his hand; for two cannot walk together, or live together, unless they be agreed. God accepts no action from an enemy but his returning to him by faith in Christ, and then begins all personal acceptance. Men must be in a state of adoption before it is possible that they can be followers of God as dear children; in a state of renovation, renewed by the Holy Ghost in the spirit of our mind. The godly man, that is in case for a godly life, is just a new creation; even the workmanship of God, created in Christ Jesus unto good works, which God before ordained that he should walk in them. If the heart be not right with God, a man cannot have a right life, or live unto God. But I shall go on to inquire,

2dly, Into the scriptural designations of this life. To give all the names that it comes under scripture, were too large a task: I shall only single out some of the most notable names it gets in scripture. —It is sometimes designed from GOD, sometimes from CHRIST, sometimes from the SPIRIT, and sometimes from these names that import the other special qualities and properties of it.

1. Sometimes it is designed from GOD ; and it is called the life of God, (Eph. 4:18), from which all natural men are alienated; this is a wonderful name that it gets, the life of God; who can tell what this life of God is? God lives in himself, and the believer lives in God: "His life is hid with Christ in God," (Col. 3:3). The best we can make of it is, that it begins in grace, and ends in glory, and is wholly in God, and in him.

2. Sometimes it is designed from CHRIST; and so it is called a living by faith on the Son of God, (Gal. 2:20), immediately following our text, where, when the apostle would explain what he understands by his living unto God, he says, "Nevertheless I live, yet not I, but Christ liveth in me." Christ, might he say, is the ALPHA and OMEGA of my life, the beginning and the end of it; the author and finisher of it; Christ is the principle of my life, from whom I live: Christ is the end of my life, to whom I live; Christ is the pattern of my life, according to whose example I live: Christ is the giver of my life, the maintainer of my life, the restorer of my life; after decays, he restores my soul, and makes me to walk in the paths of righteousness, for his name's sake: Christ is the food of my life; I would die, if he did not feed me with his flesh, which is living bread and water to me: Christ is the medicine of my life; it is by renewed touches of the hem of his garment, and renewed application to him, that my soul is healed: for, there is healing under the wings of this Sun of righteousness: Christ is the ALL of my life: "For to me to live is Christ;" he is my light, my strength, my righteousness. It is the glory of the believer to acknowledge Christ the ALPHA and the OMEGA, and the ALL of his spiritual life.

3. Sometimes it is designed from the SPIRIT, and so it is called a living in the Spirit: "If we live in the Spirit, let us also walk in the Spirit," (Gal. 5:25). It is a living in the light and leading of the Spirit; "Thy Spirit is good: lead me to the land of uprightness."—It is a living in the graces and fruits of the Spirit, which are described, (Gal. 5:22), and a bringing

forth these fruits of the Spirit.—It is a living in the strength and power of the Spirit, which is therefore called a law: "The law of the Spirit of life, in Christ Jesus, hath made me free from the law of sin and death." The power of the Spirit hath the force of a law within the man, insomuch that when he walks in the Spirit, he does not fulfill the lusts of the flesh: he sets the power of the Spirit against the power of sin. It is a living in the comforts of the Spirit, and joys of the Holy Ghost; and when he thus lives, the joy of the Lord is his strength.—It is a walking in the liberty of the Spirit; and, "Where the Spirit of the Lord is, there is liberty." When a man hath this life, then he hath liberty to hear, read, pray, believe, mourn; and liberty to serve the Lord: "Truly I am thy servant, thou hast loosed my bonds."—In a word, it is a living in the love of the Spirit, and a constant dependence on the Spirit.

4. Sometimes it is designed from these names that import other special qualities and properties of it. And here I might bring in a multitude of scriptures. It is called a holy life; "Be ye holy as I am holy."—It is a humble life; "Walk humbly with thy God." It is designed a heavenly life; "Our conversation is in heaven." The man is heavenly in his thoughts, and spiritually-minded: heavenly in his speech, desiring to edify these that are about him; heavenly in his affections, which are set on things above; his desire and delight being set upon heavenly things; heavenly in his hope; "Looking for that blessed hope, and glorious appearing of the great God:" heavenly in his trade, trading daily to the heavenly country by faith, prayer, and drawing bills of exchange upon Christ, as it were, for all that he stands in need of.—It is called an upright life; "No good thing will he withhold from him that walketh uprightly."—It is denominated a well-ordered life; "To him that orders his conversation aright, will I shew the salvation of God."—It is called a circumspect life; "See that ye walk circumspectly."—It is called a gospel life: "Let your conversation be, as it

becometh the gospel:" that is, as it becomes a gospel-state, gospel-principles, gospel-rules, gospel-patterns, gospel- motives, and gospel-ends; and, under the influence of gospel-grace, "Adorning the doctrine of God our Saviour."—But, omitting all these, I only instance in one scripture, wherein this living unto God is described, in such a manner, as includes all other properties of it; yea, and comprehends all the duties of obedience we are called to; "The grace of God that bringeth salvation, hath appeared to all men, teaching us, that denying ungodliness, and worldly lusts, we should live soberly, righteously, and godly in this present world," (Titus 2:11,12); where you see, this living unto God comprehends all these duties of piety towards God, sobriety towards ourselves, and righteousness towards our neighbor, which we are obliged to by the law, as a rule of life and holiness; and all under the influence of the grace of God, revealed in the gospel, teaching us these things efficaciously; for the law teacheth them only perceptively; but it is the gospel that teacheth them effectively; worketh in us both to will and to do. O that we knew this life more than we do.

3rdly, The third thing here was, What is imported in its being called a life in general? Indeed, this living to God is the only life that deserves the name of life. In vegetative life the trees of the field do excel men; for, from little plants they turn to stately oaks. In sensitive life the beasts of the field do excel man, for they go beyond him in these natural faculties; as the dog in smelling, the eagle in seeing, the hare in bearing, and other creatures in other senses. —In rational life many heathen philosophers may excel the Christian. So that it is not the vegetative life, whereby plants excel us, nor the sensitive life, whereby beasts excel us; nor the rational life, which reprobates have, as well as we; but the SPIRITUAL divine life, that deserves the name, without which our life is but a death. However, this spiritual life, or living to God, may be called life, because it hath all these things in it spiritually, which natural life hath in it naturally: as, 1. Life hath motion in it: and so here, this spiritual life imports motion; wherever the Spirit of life comes, there is a motion among the dry bone s.—Now, there are some duties he moves in, such as prayer; "Behold, he prayeth," who never prayed to purpose before: he moves in the duties of hearing, reading, examination and mortification.—Now, there are some graces that move in him: Faith begins to move, saying, "I believe, Lord, help mine unbelief." Hope begins to move; he is begotten to a new and lively hope. Love begins to move, maybe in sighs and groans, for want of love. Now he moves, and the term he moves from is sin, Satan, the world, self-righteousness; and the terms he moves to is God, and Christ, and heaven, and heavenly things. So far as this divine life takes place, so far all the faculties of the soul move towards God; the understanding, to see him; the will, to serve him; the affections, to embrace him: and all the members of the body move towards God; the eye is lifted up to heaven, in prayer and supplication; the ear is open to receive instruction; the mouth enlarged to sing his praises; the tongue will be no more the trumpeter of idle communication; the hand and heart will be instruments of devotion; the knees will be bowed to the God and Father of our Lord Jesus Christ; the feet will delight to carry the man to the house of the Lord; all is in motion for God, so far as this life takes place. You may here see, by the way, whether you have or want this life, which is a living to God. Though I see an image lively representing a man, having eyes, ears, mouth, nose, hands, feet, yet I know it hath no life in it, because it hath no motion; so, if we see a professor without a suitable practice, we may say he is an idol, he is no Christian, but the image of a Christian. It is true, a hypocrite may have all those external motions, like a painted puppy, that may, by some engine, be made to dance, and move up and down, but from no vital principle of life.

2. Life hath breath in it; "The body without BREATH is dead," (Jam. 2:26), as it may be rendered: so, in this life there is breath. If a man's breath be held in a little while, the person cannot live; so the believer would die if he had not breath in a spiritual sense. What is the air he breathes in? It is just the Spirit of God; "Awake, O north wind; come, thou south; blow upon my garden, that the spices thereof may flow out." What is the breath that is put within him? It is the Spirit of God: The Holy Ghost is that to the believer that breath is to the body; yea, that the soul is to the body. —God breathed into Adam the breath of life, and he breathes on the believer, saying, "Receive ye the Holy Ghost: —I will put my Spirit within you." What lungs does he breathe with? It is faith; we receive the promise of the Spirit of faith. And what things does he breathe after? Indeed, the earthly man breathes after earthly things, saying, "Who will shew us any good?" But the heavenly man breathes after heavenly things; "Lord, lift thou up the light of thy countenance upon me." Many persons have a stinking breath; it hath the smell of earth; yea, the smell of hell: Some breathe out blasphemies and oaths, some breathe out cruelty and wrath, but the man that hath this life, and lives unto God, his breath is a sweet breath; so far as he lives unto God, his breath smells of heaven, and of God, and of Christ. But, 3. Life hath usually growth; even so this life is a growing life, this well of water springs up to everlasting life. Let a painter draw the figure of grapes never so artificially, yet they may be seen and discerned from natural grapes, because they grow not: thus, the painted hypocrite may look well, but never grows. A man that hath this divine life is usually growing; if not upwardly in holiness, yet downwardly in humility; if not sensibly in outward fruitfulness, yet insensibly in inward sighs and sobs, because of his unfruitfulness; and in pantings of soul towards perfection: "He that hath clean hands waxeth stronger and stronger." Indeed, a wintertime,

or season of languishing, may put the believer far back, and interrupt the growth; but a summer-reviving will make up all again.

4. Life hath appetite and sense; even so this life imports spiritual appetite and spiritual sense; there is appetite after spiritual food. Many pamper their bodies and starve their souls, but he that thus lives hath a hunger and thirst after righteousness; and, like new-born babes, desires the sincere milk of the word, that he may grow thereby. The doctrine of the gospel is his life; for, "A man liveth not by bread alone, but by every word that proceedeth out of the mouth of God." He hath an appetite after these words of grace, and draws water with joy, out of these wells of salvation. Many are the secret longings and pantings of the living soul after the living God, who is his life; and, as life seeks its living soul continually, so does the living soul in the living God, in whom only his life is hid.—There is sense also: here life is sensible of whatsoever is an enemy to it, and resists it; the more life, the more sense; and the more sense, the more resistance: even so, they that live this life unto God, they feel corruption, and they fight against it; For the Spirit lusts against the flesh, and the flesh against the Spirit;" they groan under the weight of corruption which they feel, and reckon themselves wretched on the account thereof; "O wretched man that I am! who shall deliver me from the body of this death?" They that have no feeling of sin, no fighting against it, do look like these that have this life.—They who have spiritual senses, at least who have them exercised, they have the seeing eye, they see the evil of sin, they see the beauty of holiness, they see the glory of God in the face of Jesus Christ, they see God in his ordinances, they see an internal glory in the external administration of ordinances, which, others not seeing, they think very little of these things: also, they see God in his providences; in his judgments they see a just God, and in mercies they see a merciful God, and themselves less than the least of all

his mercies.—They have the hearing ear; they hear the voice of God in the word, and rod: they, smell the savor of his name, which is as ointment poured forth: they taste his goodness, and feel his power.—And thus you see what may be imported in its being called a life in general.

4thly, The fourth thing was, What is imported in its being called a living unto God: what is this living unto God? I have said several things about it already; but this living unto God, more particularly, may import these four things following.

1. The believer's living unto God imports his living suitably to the relations that God stands in to him, and he unto God, as being his God in Christ Jesus; and so it is a living to him as our Redeemer, both by price and power; as these that are not our own, but bought with a price; and therefore glorifying the Lord in our souls and bodies, which are his. It is a living to God as our Head: God in Christ is the believer's Head, and so, to live to him as our Head is to live as members of such a Head, drawing spiritual virtue, light, life, and comfort from him as the Head.

It is a living to God as our Husband; "Thy Maker is thy Husband;" and so to live to him in this relation, is to live reverently, lovingly, affectionately, with submission and subjection to our Husband, as becomes the spouse of such a glorious Husband. It is a living to God as our heavenly Father, depending on him as children on their father; "Wilt thou not, from this time, call me, My Father, thou art the guide of my youth?" (Jer. 3:4). It is a living to God as our Judge, Law-giver, and King; and so it is as living as these that are accountable to, and as we shall answer at the tribunal of this impartial Judge: it is a sitting at the feet, and receiving the law from the mouth of this righteous Lawgiver: and it is a yielding the tribute of praise, obedience, and subjection to this almighty King.—In a word, it is a living to God as the object of our worship and adoration;

loving him as the Lord our God, with all our heart, soul, mind, and strength.—

Thus, I say, to live to God is to live suitably to all these relations he stands in to us.

2. The believer's living unto God imports his living suitably to these privileges and favors that he receives from God. —Hath he enlightened us in the knowledge of himself? Then, to live to him is to walk as children of light, and not as those that are yet in darkness and ignorance. —Hath he called us effectually? Then, to live to him is to walk worthy of the vocation wherewith we are called. —Hath he given us grace? Then, to live to him is to live, not as graceless, but as gracious persons; not as those that are in a state of nature, but in a state of grace. —Hath he pardoned our sins, justified our persons, and brought us into peace with himself? Then, to live to him is to stand fast in the liberty wherewith he hath made us free. —Hath he renewed and sanctified us?

Then, to live to him is to live as renewed and sanctified persons, whose lusts are mortified, and whose souls are transformed into the image of God. —Hath he poured in the promise into our hearts by the Spirit? Then, to live unto him suitably thereunto is, having these promises, to cleanse ourselves from the filthiness of the flesh, and of the spirit, perfecting holiness in the fear of God. —Hath he made us heirs of glory? Then, to live to him is to live as candidates for heaven; as pilgrims and strangers abstaining from fleshly lusts; travelling to the other world, having our affections and conversation in heaven.

3. The believer's living unto God, imports, his living in communion with him, and comfortable enjoyment of him: In communion with him; in the contemplation of him; sanctifying the Lord in our hearts: in a constant affection to him; having his love shed abroad in our hearts, by the Holy Ghost: and in a constant dependence on him; receiving all from

him by faith, and returning all to him in duty and gratitude. It is a living in the comfortable enjoyment of him, as all our portion and happiness, all our salvation and desire; renouncing all things in heaven and earth as our portion, but a God in Christ alone, saying, "Whom have I in heaven but thee? and there is none in all the earth that I desire besides thee."

4. The believer's living unto God, imports, his living in conformity to God; and, indeed, so far as we enjoy God, so far will we be conformed to him. As it will be in glory, "We shall be like him, for, we shall see him as he is:" so it is in grace here: the more the soul sees and enjoys him, the more is he like unto him; "Beholding his glory, we are changed into the same image, from glory to glory." And so this living unto God, it is a living in conformity to God's nature; being holy as he is holy; perfect as our heavenly Father is perfect.

Is he a perfect God? Then to live to him, is to go on to perfection, (Heb. 6:1). It is a living in conformity to his way of living: God's way of living is a holy, just, good, faithful, merciful way; having a general goodwill to all, and a special goodwill to some; and so ought our ways to be. It is a living in conformity to God's ends: God's great end, that he sets before himself, is the glory of his name, the honor of his Son, the advancement of Christ's kingdom, the ruin of Satan's kingdom, and in all, the praise of his rich and free grace: and surely we live to God, when we have these ends also which are God's ends. It is a living in conformity to his law as a rule, which is the transcript of his communicable nature, for our practice; "If ye love me, keep my commandments;" we do not love him, if we do not so. They then that live to him, they do, from love as well as conscience, obey him. These things night be greatly enlarged; however, thus you see in short, what it is to live unto God. We are telling, and you are hearing, what this life is; but, O that we could live this life, as well as speak and hear of it! Look to the Lord, that he may make you know it to your experience. It is called a living to God,

1. Because it hath the Spirit of God for the principle of it.

2. Because it hath the word of God for the rule of it.

3. Because it hath the love of God for the motive of it. And

4. Because it hath the glory of God for the ultimate end of it.

CHAPTER 7

The Necessity of this death, in order to this life

T he Fourth thing proposed was, to show the INFLUENCE that this being dead to the law, hath upon living to God; or the NE-CESSITY of this death, in order to this life. Here I might shew,

1. That it is necessary.

2. Whence it is necessary.

1st, That it is necessary that we die to the law, in point of justification, before we can live to God in point of sanctification: besides what was said upon the first head, for the confirmation of the doctrine, these following considerations, or remarks, may discover the necessity of being dead to the law, in order to our living to God.

1. Remark, That a man that is under the law, can perform no holy act: he may do some things that are materially good, but nothing can he do that is formally good, or holy: and his work, instead of sanctifying him, does still more and more pollute him; "To the pure all things are pure; but unto them that are defiled, and unbelieving, is nothing pure; but even their mind and conscience is defiled," (Titus 1:5). He then that is

alive to the law, and under the covenant of works, his works can never make him holy, but rather more and more unholy.

2. Remark, The man that is under the law, hath no promise of holiness or sanctification by that law. The law only promises life, upon perfect obedience, in our own person; and if true sanctification may be in one that is under the covenant of works, then we must change the articles of the covenant, and promises of the covenant of grace, and make sanctification no promise of it: we must blot out these promises, "I will put a new Spirit within you, and, I will write my law in your hearts:" and all other promises of the like nature, must be razed out of the covenant of grace: If one under the covenant of works may attain to sanctification by his own works, there is no need of this promise.

3. Remark, That the man that is under the law, hath no principle of holiness. The grand principle of true holiness, is the Spirit dwelling in the man; now, how does one receive the Spirit of sanctification? "Is it by the works of the law? No; but by the hearing of faith," (Gal. 3:2). It is the doctrine of grace, not of works, that makes us partake of this Spirit. It is the New Testament, or new covenant, that is the manifestation of the Spirit, (2 Cor. 3:2). Thereby the Spirit is ministered, or conveyed to us, but not by the law. It is the gospel that calls us effectually to sanctification, (2 Thess. 2:13,14). We received the promise of the Spirit through faith, and not by the works of the law, (Gal. 3:14).

4. Remark, That the man that is under the law, is without Christ, in whom sanctification only is to be found; they that are saints, are saints in Christ Jesus, as the apostle designs them; and sanctified in Christ: and our implantation into Christ, is only from grace, and only in Christ, who gave himself for his church, that he might sanctify it, (Eph. 5:25).

5. Remark, the man that is under the law, is without strength, and cannot perform obedience to the law: the law is weak through the flesh,

and cannot justify him, neither can it sanctify him. In order to sanctification, a new creation is necessary: the clean heart must be created; and the man created unto good works; creating power must be put forth; and creation is a work of God. We must therefore make a God of our works, and deify, them, and endow them with a creating power, if we think, by the works of the law, to be sanctified; or ascribe such efficacy to them, as to work true sanctification in us. No man, then, that is under the law, or covenant of works, by giving himself to all holy duties and actions, and exercising himself in them, can come to attain true holiness, or to be truly sanctified.

6. Remark, That the man that is under the power of the law, is under the power of sin. Whence is it, that the believer is freed from the power and dominion of sin? It is because he is under grace, and not under the law, (Rom. 6:14). Showing us, that these that are under the law, are under the power and dominion of sin. How so? Even upon the account of all reasons already assigned; and not only so, but because the law is the strength of sin, (1 Cor. 15:56). Particularly as it irritates corruption, strengthening and stirring it up; "Sin taking occasion by the commandment, wrought in me all manner of concupiscence." Sin, by occasion of the resisting command, brake out the more fiercely. Hence the law is only the occasion, and sin dwelling in us the cause; as the shining of the sun is the occasion, why a dung-hill sends forth its filthy savor, it is the corruption and putrefaction therein that is the cause; so here, the light of the law shining, and discovering sin and duty, is the occasion of sin's irritation and increase, but corruption itself is the cause. Well, so it is, that a man being under the law, is under the power of sin; how then can he live unto God, while under the law? or, how can sanctification take place while he is alive to the law, or not dead thereto?—These things may make it evident, I think, that it is necessary, that a man be dead to the law,

and brought from under it, before he can have true satisfaction, or live unto God.

2dly, Whence it is necessary, that a man be dead to the law in point of justification, in order to his living to God in point of sanctification: These particulars already mentioned, afforded so many reasons of the necessity thereof: yet some things more may be said, for the further clearing of this point, namely, The influence that dying to the law, hath upon our living unto God. Here two questions occur. 1. What influence living TO the law, hath upon a man's living IN sin. 2.

What influence a man's dying TO the law, hath upon his dying to sin, and living UNTO God.

1. What influence a man's living TO the law, or being alive to the law, hath upon his living IN sin.—This is a strange doctrine, some may think; but it is as true as strange, that the law, and our works of obedience to the law, while we are under it, is the cause of destruction, instead of salvation, (Rom. 9:31,32). There you see it destroyed the whole Jewish nation; "Israel missed righteousness, because they sought it by the works of the law."—Now a man's being alive to the law, hath influence upon his living in sin, and so upon his destruction, in the following ways: —

1. Because hereby he becomes hardened in sin and security, while he thinks he hath some good work to bear him out, (Prov. 7:14). What made the filthy whore more impudent and hardened in her sins? Why? "I have peace-offerings with me; this day I have paid my vows." Thus the Pharisees, for a pretense, made long prayers; and hereupon were hardened in their sinful courses, fearless of wrath: Why, I have done so and so.

2. Hereby they are kept from Christ, who only saves from sin. The works of the law step in betwixt them and Christ, and the man takes Christ's bargain off his hand, promising the same that Christ promised,

even obedience to the law: "I delight to do thy will," says Christ; nay, I will do it myself, says the man that is under the law: he makes himself his own saviour.—What! will not God accept of my good and honest endeavors? This is what he sets up on Christ's throne; and if Christ be pulled down from his throne, will it be sufficient that we set up an honest prince in his room; They have some things to say for themselves, which, they hope, will bring them off before God. Thus they reject Christ, "The Lamb of God, who takes away the sins of the world;" and how can then but live unto sin, whatever they may think of themselves?

3. Hereby their pride and boasting is fostered, "To him that worketh, is the reward not reckoned of grace, but of debt," (Rom. 4:4). And the man expects his due for his work, which he glories in; for, "Boasting is not excluded by the law of works," (Rom. 3:27). And therefore, the man is loath to part with his own righteousness, which is by the law: because of his pride, he will not stoop to live upon another, while he can shift for himself. Self-love will not suffer a man to think the worst of himself, so long as he is alive to the law: nay, I hope: I have a good heart to God, and I will do something that will please God; and so it is no little thing will bring him to submit to the righteousness of God, (Rom. 10:3). Thus, the law fosters his pride; and sure the proud man was never a holy man. But,

4. Hereby sin is strengthened and increased, as I said before: the motions of sin are by the law, (Rom. 7:5); "The law entered, that sin might abound," (Rom. 5:20). Not only as to the knowledge of it, which is by the law, but as to the actual out-breaking of it from the heart; like a river being bounded and dammed up by the law, it swells and breaks out the more violently. The wicked nature of man, being reproved, swells and rises like a snake brought to the fire.

5. Hereby the man becomes desperate; for the law says, There is no hope without a perfect obedience; and the man having wearied himself in doing nothing answerable to what the law requires, comes at last, perhaps, to see there is no hope, and so he dies in despair; I mean, he dies in sin, saying, There is no hope; and therefore after idols I will go; he flies away from God, as Adam did.

6. Hereby he becomes slavish also; the fear, torment, and wrath, which the law brings along with it, when the penalty of it is seen, weakens the man's hands; and these lying like heavy loads upon the soul, it is thereby fettered and bound in prison, hence said to be held in the law; "That being dead wherein we were held," says the apostle. The man is held, and shut up in the prison of the law, and so out of case for service while his bands are not loosed; or at best his service is slavish, and not free; the law holds him in prison, he cannot serve God freely. The free Spirit of the gospel is what the world cannot receive, while under the law. Thus, you may see what influence living to the law may have upon men's living in sin, so as they cannot live unto God.

(2.) What influence a man's dying To the law hath upon his living UNTO God, or upon holiness and sanctification? To this we reply, It hath especially a twofold influence, both a physical and moral influence. —And,[1.] It hath a physical influence upon a man's sanctification, in regard that a man that is dead to the law, is married to Christ, (Rom. 7:4); and so necessarily the man must be holy, being disjoined from the law, and joined to the Lord Jesus, who hath satisfied the precept of the law by his death: and in him, not only have they thus a full discharge of all the demands and commands of the law, but also, by the implantation and inhabitation of his Spirit, are created to a conformity to the image of God; and they cannot but live unto God. For,

1. In Christ they have life; though, while under the law, they were dead in sin and trespasses; now, in Christ, they have life, and have it more abundantly: they are quickened by virtue of their union to this everlasting Head; because he lives, they live also. A dead person can produce no living action, but Christ is the life of his people: "He that hath the Son hath life:" and then, and never till then, is he in case for spiritual action and living unto God: "He that hath not the Son of God, hath not life." Vain men fancy within themselves, that they have not lost their life, and so they think they can do something that will please God, and profit themselves for justification and sanctification, even before ever they think of coming to Christ; but we may as well expect, that a dead corpse will rise of itself and do the natural actions of life, as to expect that you should rise, and act spiritually, before you be in Christ. The natural conscience indeed may be roused a little, and prevailed with to set about this and that duty; but there is no living unto God, till you get Christ: in him the believer hath life, even in his Head; as a man cannot live without his head; but, being joined to this new head, and disjoined from the law, he cannot but live.

2. In Christ, his new Head and Husband, he hath light as well as life: as you know, the eye is in the head, so the believer's eye is in Christ his light, whereby he sees sin and duty; sees to work, so as he may live to God. The man that is under the law, he is in the dark, and cannot see to work the works of holiness, which is a living unto God. He is blinded with self-conceit; he sees not the vanity of his old covenant obedience; and he sees not the way of the new covenant gospel-obedience, till he get the Spirit of wisdom and revelation in the knowledge of Christ, who is the light of the world; a light to lighten the Gentiles: by whose light the believer sees how to walk in a way well-pleasing to God.

3. In Christ, his new Head, he hath strength: the man that is under the law, joined to it as his Head, he hath no strength for his work, and the law gives him none; and so he cannot live to God; but the believer can say, "In the Lord have I righteousness and strength;" whereas others have no strength to produce spiritual actions; sin domineers over them, and they have no ability to shake off the poke of sin, their strength being, but weakness. The believer hath strength in his head; all things are possible to them that believe; they can do all things through Christ strengthening them; they can overleap a wall, and break bows of steel in pieces. O, believer, be strong in the grace that is in Christ. O, it is strange the grace that is in him is in thee; as the life that is in the heart, is in the toe, the foot, the utmost members! There is a communication of vital strength and influences from the heart and head to all the members; the believer's grace is in Christ, and the grace that is in Christ is in the believer. Here is a mystery to the world but yet this mystery lies wrapt up in that word, "Be strong in the grace that is in Christ Jesus." If the grace that is in Christ, were not in the believer also, according to the measure of the communication, how could he be strong in the grace that is in Christ? "My grace shall be sufficient for thee, and my strength shall be perfect in thy weakness."

4. In Christ, his new Head, he hath liberty: under the law the man is under bondage, and severe bondage to the command of perfect obedience, upon pain of death and damnation; and so under bondage to the curse of the law, and fear of God's everlasting wrath and thereby he can do nothing; he hath neither heart nor hand to serve God; he is bound neck and heel, but in Christ he hath liberty; "If the Son make you free, you are free indeed;" free from service; "Truly I am thy servant, thou hast loosed my bands." Now, he walks at liberty, yea, runs the way of God's commandments, when he doth enlarge his heart. This is the glorious

liberty of the children of God begun in time, whereby they are put in case to live unto God.—Now, he is at liberty to serve cheerfully, being delivered from the hands of all his enemies, to serve him without fear, in holiness and righteousness, all the days of his life.—Now, he is at liberty to serve spiritually; the Spirit of Christ being put within him, and causing him to walk in God's statutes.—Now, he is at liberty to serve hopefully, knowing that his labor shall not be in vain in the Lord; though, while under the law, his labor was but vain labor.—Now, he is at liberty to serve acceptably, being accepted in the Beloved, (Eph. 1:6), that is, not only for his sake; for there is much more in it, he being our Head, and we members of his body; and he, as our Head, having performed perfect obedience to the precept of the law, and given complete satisfaction to the penalty of the law; the Head having done it, the whole body is reputed as having done it, and so we are accepted in him; his doing is ours, because we are in him, as our Head, accepted in the Beloved; our persons are accepted in him, and next our performances and duties. O, what sweet liberty is here! what a sweet foundation for spiritual and acceptable service and living unto God! But this leads me, next, to show,

[2.] That it hath a moral influence upon sanctification; a man's being dead to the law, disjoined from it, and joined to Christ, hath not only a physical, but also a moral influence; in regard that hereby he is constrained sweetly to live unto God; "The love of Christ constraineth us," (2 Cor. 5:14,15). If we have not love at the root of our actions, love to a God in Christ, we are but empty vines, that bring forth fruit to ourselves; it is but self-love, which is not fruit unto God, or living unto him. The natural way of man's thinking is, we should serve God, that he may save us; but the gospel-way is, he saves us, that we may save him. What made Paul say, "Being dead to the law, I live unto God?" Why, in the next verse he enlarges on it; "I live to him who loved me and gave himself for me."

Be persuaded, man, woman, of this, or else, as the Lord lives, you shall die in a delusion; that, if you have not love to God, you have not a spark of holiness, though you should pray all your days, and work never so hard; "I will circumcise their hearts to love me," is the promise, and this love is the heart and life of religious duties.—Now, you cannot have love unless you see somewhat more or less of his love to you; we are naturally enemies to God, though we cannot get one of a thousand that will take with it; they think they have a love to God.

God forbid, say they, that we should be enemies; nay, but I tell you, in the name of God, whether you will hear it or not, that, as you are enemies by nature, and born with a dagger of enmity in your heart and hand against God, so, till you get somewhat of the knowledge of God, as in Christ reconciling the world to himself, this enmity will never be killed. Now, I say it is the believer in Christ who, being dead to the law, and joined to the Lord, hath this love; and this love constrains him, so that he brings forth fruit unto God, and lives unto him, (Rom. 7:3); being dead to the law, and married to Christ, he brings forth fruit unto God. The believer hath sufficient encouragement to make him live unto God; he sees Christ hath satisfied divine justice, fulfilled all the righteousness of the law, that he hath done that which is impossible, or unperformable by us; and when, by faith, he beholds this, he is encouraged to serve God. Hence, says the psalmist, "There is mercy with thee, that thou mayest be feared."—Might he not have said, there is majesty with thee, that thou mayest be feared? The matter is, the majesty of God would put the sinner to flee from God, as Adam did when he heard his voice in the garden; but his mercy makes us fear and love him, serve and obey him; "Then they shall fear the Lord and his goodness," says the prophet, (Hosea 3:5). If a man hath no faith at all of God's goodness, no hope of his favor in Christ, where is his purity and holiness? Nay, it is he that hath this hope, that purifies himself, as he is pure. I know not what experience you have, sirs, but some of us know that, when our souls are most comforted and enlarged with the faith of God's favor through Christ, and with the hope of his goodness, then we have most heart to the duties; and when, through unbelief, we have harsh thoughts of God as an angry judge, then we have no heart to duties and religious exercises: and I persuade myself this is the experience of the saints in all ages.

But, that this moral influence, which, dying to the law, or covenant of works, hath upon living to God, or holiness and sanctification, may be further evident: let us consider how the law to the believer, having now lost its legal or old covenant form, and being put into a gospel-form, and changed from the law of works into a covenant of grace, or the law in the hand of Christ; how, I say, every part of it now constrains the believer to obedience and sanctification, in a most loving manner. The gospel-law, or the law of grace, that now he is under, is a chariot paved with love.

The law, in the hand of Christ, hath now another face, even a smiling face, in all the commands, promises, threatenings, and in the whole form thereof.

(1.) The commands of the law, in the hand of Christ, have lost their old covenant-form, and are full of love. The command of the law of works is Do, and Live; but in the hand of Christ, it is, Live, and Do: the command of the law of works, is, Do, or else be damned: but the law in the hand of Christ is, I have delivered thee from hell, therefore DO: the command of the law of works is, Do in thy own strength; but the law in the hand of Christ is, "I am thy strength: My strength shall be perfected in thy weakness," therefore Do. The command is materially the same, but the form is different: the command or the law of works is, Do perfectly, that you may have eternal life; but now, in the hand of Christ, the form is, I have given thee eternal life in me, and by my doing; and therefore do as perfectly as you can, through my grace, till you come to a state of perfection. The command, I say, is the same materially; for I do not join with these, who insinuate, as if here less obedience were required than under the law of works; though less be accepted in these who have a perfect obedience in their Head, yet no less is required, though not in the old covenant-form. And as the command is materially the same, so the authority enjoining obedience is originally the same, yet vastly distinct: in that the command of the law is the command of God out of Christ, an absolute God and Judge: but now, under grace, it is the command of a God in Christ, a Father in him: and sure I am, that the authority of the commanding God is not lessened, or lost, that the command is now in the hand of Christ: Christ is God, coequal and coessential with the Father: and as God's authority to judge is not lost, or lessened, in that all judgment is committed to the Son; so his authority to command, is not lost or lessened, in that the law is in the hand of Christ: nay, it is not lessened, but it is sweetened, and made amiable, lovely, and desirable to the believer, constraining him to obedience, in that the law is in the hand of his Head, his Lord, and his God.—The end that he hath in commanding, and that they should have in obeying, is now distinct, and different from what took place under the law of works: the end that he hath in commanding, is not to lay a heavy yoke of duties on their necks, to be borne by their own strength: nor, though performed by his strength, to be a righteousness for their justification, or a condition of life; but only to show his holy nature, that he will not have a lawless people; to show his great grace, that condescends to seek our service; to show grace and beautify his people, their chief happiness consisting in a conformity to his will; that his people may get good, which is necessarily joined to duties, and connected thereto by the promises; that he may have something to commend his people for; and that he may, without a compliment, have ground to say, "Well done, good and faithful servants:" and that by them he may have matter of condemnation against the rest of the world, who walk not in his commandments. In a word, he commands that his sovereignty may be kept up, and the sense thereof, in the hearts of his people: and that, by his word of command, he may, as many times as he doth, convey strength to do what he calls to; and in case of short-coming, to force them out of themselves, under a sense of weakness and sinfulness, into Jesus Christ, the end of the law, for strength to sanctify, as well as for righteousness to justify. For these, and such like ends, does the Lord command.—And then the end that they should have in obeying, is not to satisfy conscience, nor to satisfy justice, to purchase heaven, or the like; but to glorify God, to edify our neighbor, and to testify our gratitude to God, and Christ, that hath delivered us from the law, as a covenant.

(2.) The promises of the law, in the hand of Christ, have lost their old covenant-form, and are full of love. The law of works promises eternal life, as a reward of our doing, or obedience; and here the reward is a reward of debt; but the law, in the hand of Christ, promises a reward of grace to gospel-obedience, especially as it is as evidence of union to him, in whom all the promises are Yea and Amen. Eternal life was promised in the covenant of redemption to Christ, upon his perfect obedience, who paid that debt when he came under the law of works for us; and now, eternal life being obtained to the believer in Christ, as the reward of Christ's obedience to the death, there is no other reward of debt than now takes place.—Rewards of grace are now come in fashion, and this encourages the believer to live unto God, that in the way of gospel-obedience, there is a gracious promise of sweet communion and fellowship with God; "He that loves me, and keeps my commandments; I will love him, and manifest myself to him, and my Father will love him," (John 14:21). Here there is a fatherly promise of God's favor and familiarity with him; yea there is a promise of heaven itself in the way of gospel-obedience, and sanctification: a right to heaven is purchased by the blood of Christ, and the believer is the young heir of glory: but his possession of heaven is suspended till he be fit for it; till he do some business for his Father, and be made meet for the inheritance of the saints in light. This is sweet encouragement the believer hath, to live unto God.

(3) The threatenings of the law, in the hand of Christ, have lost their old covenant-form, quality, and nature, and are now turned to threatenings out of love; there is no such threatening now to the believer, If thou do not, thou shalt die. The penalty of the law of works is condemnation and eternal death, which the believer hath no cause to fear, being dead to the law; no more than a living wife needs to fear the threatenings of her dead husband: "There is no condemnation to them that are in Christ. He that believes in him, shall never die." Believers are under no threatening of external wrath, because [they are] under grace. It is a high expression that blessed Rutherford hath to this purpose, "The gospel, says he, forbids nothing under pain of damnation to a justified believer, more than to Jesus Christ."—Though the sins of believers deserve hell, and the intrinsic demerit of sin is still the same; [yea, I think the sins of believers being against so much love, and so many mercies, they deserve a thousand hells, where others deserve one;] yet, being dead to the law, he hath no vindictive wrath to fear, the blood of Christ having quenched the fire of God's wrath, "While we were sinners, Christ died for us; and much more now being justified by his blood, we are saved from wrath through him," (Rom. 5:9); and sure he is not to fear that which God calls him to believe he is saved from: his slavish fear, therefore, is from unbelief, and weakens his hands in duties But now the law, in the hand of Christ, hath theatenings and punishments, but they are fatherly and

loving: a short view of them you may read, "If his children forsake my law, and walk not in my judgments: if they break my statutes, and keep not my commandments, then will I visit their transgression with the rod, and their iniquities with stripes; nevertheless, my loving-kindness will I not utterly take from him, nor suffer my faithfulness to fail; my covenant will I not break.—Once have I sworn by my holiness, that I will not lie unto David," (Ps. 89:30-35). Though I will not send them to hell, nor deprive them of heaven, no more than I will break my great oath to my eternal Son; yet, like a father, I will chastise them; I will correct them for their faults: I will squeeze them in the mortar of affliction, and press out the corrupt juice of old Adam that is in them; yea, I will hide my face: I will deny them that communion and fellowship with me that sometimes they had, and give them terror instead of comfort, and bitterness instead of sweetness. A filial tear of these fatherly chastisements will do more to influence the believer to holiness and obedience, than all the unbelieving fears of hell and wrath can do: fear, lest he want that sweetness of God's presence, which sometimes he hath had, will make him say to his sins and lusts, as the fig-tree in Jotham's parable, "Shall I leave my sweetness, and be king over you?" O! shall I leave all the sweetness that I have enjoyed with God and take on with base lusts and idols! And hence, when the believer hath gone aside and backslidden, what is it that brings him back to God? He finds the Lord breaking him many ways, and he reflects, through grace, upon this sometimes. O! How am I deprived of these sweet interviews that once I enjoyed? "Therefore, I will go and return to my first husband, for then it was better with me than now." Yea, his freedom from law-threatenings, and being only under fatherly correction, when he sees this, it breaks his heart, and melts it more than all the fire of hell could do.—The slavish fear of vindictive wrath discourages him, weakens his hands in duties, and makes him run away from God:

but the filial fear of God's fatherly wrath, which is kindly, is a motive of love that encourages him to his duty. Which of these motives think you will work up the believer to most obedience? viz. This legal one, O! my wrathful Judge will send me to hell, if I do so and so; or this gospel one; O! my God and Father in Christ Jesus will be angry at me, and deny me his love-tokens? I suppose the former works upon enmity, and raises it, but this works upon love, and inflames it.

But here a question may be moved, ought not the believer to live unto God, even without respect to the threatening of fatherly chastisement and punishment? To this we answer, no doubt, the more perfect his obedience be, the better and the more like to the obedience of the saints in heaven, where no chastisement is feared; but, while he is here, he carries a body of sin about with him, and needs to be stirred up by fatherly correction. He should indeed serve God purely out of love and respect to the command itself, and because he commands it; but thus the matter stands, that as on the one hand, being perfect in his Head, Christ Jesus, it is not his duty to have respect to what the law of works either promises, or threatens; so, on the other hand, being imperfect in himself while here, it is his duty to have respect to what the law, in the hand of Christ, promises and threatens; which indeed is a loving respect, tending to advance holiness.

(4.) The whole form of the law, as a covenant of works, being thus altered, the law in the hand of Christ, is all love, all grace, and so influences the man to sanctification. The man that is under the covenant of grace, he hath a principle of grace within him, causing him to walk in God's statutes; he hath the promise of grace to be sufficient for him; if sin prevail, and pollute him, he hath daily access to the fountain open for sin and for uncleanness, to which he runs; if his backslidings increase, he hath Christ engaged by promise to heal his backslidings: which, when he views by faith, it doth not encourage him to sin, if he be in right exercise of his senses, but draws him to his duty, like a cord of love, and brings him back to his kind Lord. In a word, being dead to the law, he is married to Christ, who is like a green fig-tree, from whom all his fruit is found. —Thus you see what influence a man's being dead to the law, hath upon his living unto God. And so much for the fourth head proposed.

CHAPTER 8

Application

The Fifth thing in the method was the Application, which we shall essay in an Use of Information, Examination, Lamentation, and Exhortation.

Is it so, that being dead to the law, in point of justification, is necessary, in order to living unto God in point of sanctification? Then for Information, hence we may see,

1. That the doctrine of the gospel is not a doctrine of licentiousness, or carnal liberty, however it be reproached in the world: and if the preachers thereof, who would bring people from the law of works, and from their self-righteousness, be reproached as if they were enemies to holiness I will venture to say it with confidence, in a place where falsehood should be an abomination, that it is a vile slander; for whatever sinful weakness and imperfection may cleave to the preaching or practice of these, who desire to publish this gospel-doctrine, yet the Lord God of gods is witness; yea, the Lord God of gods knows, and all Israel may know, and all whose eyes God enlightens shall know, that this doctrine of dying to the law, in point of justification, is a doctrine according to godliness, and the very means

of holiness itself, and of living unto God: if this be Antinomianism, I am content to be called an Antinomian. 1 But, we see, who are indeed Antinomians, and enemies to the law and holiness; even all those who oppose this doctrine, whereby we give the law all the honor imaginable; "Do we make void the law through faith; God forbid; yea, we establish the law:" as a covenant we establish it, while we preach Christ as our righteousness for justification: and as a rule of holiness we establish it, while we preach Christ as our strength for sanctification of heart and life: and they that do not thus honor the law, do but disgrace and dishonor it, and are truly Antinomians, i.e. enemies to the law. And if this be called a new scheme of doctrine, by way of reproach, though I confess it is a new covenant scheme, in opposition to that of the old, yet I will grant to no man that it is new otherwise; seeing it is not only as old as Paul here, but as old as the first publication of the covenant of grace in Paradise; so that we see where it is, that the reproach of a new scheme should be lodged.—I would have reproachers to mind what Paul says of this doctrine of his, "If we, or an angel from heaven, preach another gospel, let him be accursed," (Gal. 1:8). Here is the doom of such as preach another gospel, which yet, says the apostle, is not another; but there are some that trouble the Lord's people, and would pervert the gospel of Christ. To be dead to the law, is not to turn a loose Antinomian; it is to live unto God.

2. Hence see the reason why the devil opposes the doctrine of grace so much, and cares not though the law, as a covenant, be never so much preached up, because it is the gospel-doctrine that tends only to true godliness, while the law and legal doctrines tend to keep men strangers to the life of God. The devil cares not how much you be in duties, providing you keep off from Christ, who is the end of the law, for righteousness: for then he knows you would be holy also: but he is an unholy devil; and therefore, he opposes the gospel, and its doctrine. The devil knows that

he hath fast hold of you, so long as you cleave to the law; but that he hath lost you, if once you have laid hold on Christ: for, if once you get Christ for justification, as having fulfilled the righteousness of the law for you, then you will also get him for sanctification, to fulfill the righteousness of the law in you. The devil knows, that though in seeming holiness, you should be transformed to an angel of light, like himself, yet you lie under the heavy vengeance of God, and curse of the law, and under the power of sin too, so long as you are under the law. Therefore,

3. Hence see the reason why most parts of the world are living to sin, living to self, living to the world, living to the devil: Why? because they are not dead to the law. They only that are dead to the law, do live unto God: and surely then, they that are alive to the law, and not dead to it, they are living to the devil. No man that is alive to the law, can be a holy man; nay, what is the reason of all the ungodliness and unrighteousness, all the profanity and wickedness of the generation!

Why? people are strangers to Christ and are still under the power, the irritating power of the law, which is the strength of sin. The world is crying up morality, as if the preachers of Christ and his righteousness were enemies to the moral law, as a rule of holiness; and behold, in the righteous judgment of God, there was never a generation left to greater immoralities than the present; a just punishment of men's despising Christ, and his law-biding righteousness, through the faith whereof only true holiness, and conformity to the law can be attained. O when the believer comes to see by faith, that he hath nothing to do with the law as a covenant, this makes him delight in the law of God, as a rule of holiness; when he sees he hath not a farthing of debt to pay, either to the precept, or threatening of the law as a covenant, because that debt was paid by Christ's obedience to the death, this makes him find himself under the most grateful obligations to serve the Lord, in obedience to his law, as a rule; yea, under greater obligation than ever Adam was in the state of innocency; but the rest of the world that are utter strangers to this freedom, they are in bondage to the law, and so in bondage to their lusts.

4. Hence we may see the necessity of a law-work of conviction and humiliation, and how much of it is necessary, even as much as will render the person dead to the law, that he may live unto God. So much conviction is necessary, as will unbottom the man from the covenant of works, and make him disclaim his own righteousness, and make him cry out, "Unclean, unclean;" guilty, guilty; that thus his self-confidence may be killed, and he, through the law, may be dead to the law, and may come under the cover of the blood of the Lamb, under cover of the righteousness of Christ for justification that, being dead to the law, he may live unto God. While men are without this law work, rendering them dead to the law, they are at best but establishing a righteousness of their own, which will keep them out of heaven, as much as their sins will do.

And this makes the gate of heaven indeed to be a strait gate because many seek to enter in, in a legal way, and shall not be able, (Luke 13:24); and this makes the broad way that leads unto hell, so broad, that it lets in all that are out of Christ, but the openly wicked, and the self-righteous.

There is but one way to heaven, and that is Christ; but there are many ways to hell: especially these two; some walk in a more cleanly way of self-righteousness, and others in a more dirty way of open wickedness; but both meet together at the end of the way, and that is the centre of damnation. O what need, then, is there of a law-work, to convince the wicked of their sins, and the self-righteous of their need of a better righteousness, that, being dead to the law, they may live unto God.

5. Hence we may see, whence it is, that believers live so little to God, and are so untender, and unholy: it flows from this, that they are not perfectly dead to the law, nor perfectly freed from it: much of a legal spirit remains; the more that takes place, the more unholy they are. Though they have shaken off, in conversion, the authority of the covenant of works as a prince, which is a great matter; yet they are many times under the authority thereof as an usurper, and by reason of the old legal nature, which is but partly renewed in time; and hence the voice of the law speaks many times in the believer's conscience, and he is terrified at the voice of it; for it presumes to curse him, and to desire him to do, or else be damned; and so it weakens his hand, and makes him think God is a hard master: whereas the voice of the gospel in his conscience, is the still, calm voice, sweetly entreating, and alluring the heart to its obedience, and conveying a secret strength to obey, and making the soul to delight in the Lord's way; "Draw me, we will run after thee," (Song 1:3). But what should the believer do, when the law comes to charge him, and command him to obey upon pain of death, or to curse him for his disobedience? Why, he may even say in the words of Luther, who, upon the point of justification, was as sound as any since his day; "O law, Christ is my righteousness, my treasure, and my work; I confess, O law, that I am neither godly nor righteous, but yet this I am sure of, that he is godly and righteous for me."

His obedience answered both the godliness required in the first table of the law, and the righteousness required in the second table. The believer may say to the law, O law, I am dead to thee, and married to another Husband, even Jesus Christ; and therefore, cannot bring forth any children, any fruit, any acts of obedience to thy threatening commands: but, behold, I run to my sweet husband, who hath sugared and sweetened the law, with a gospel-dress and form; which, giving strength to obey, and showing the believer's freedom from the wrath of God, "encourages the believer, as our Confession of Faith speaks, being free from the curse of the moral law, and delivered from everlasting damnation, to yield obedience to God;" not out of slavish fear, but a child-like love, and a willing mind.

6. Hence see how it is, that holiness is necessary to salvation why, it is the very life of the justified man, being dead to the law, to live unto God: he is not holy that he may be justified, but justified that he may be holy. I do not here meddle with the question, whether regeneration or justification be first in order of nature? For I am speaking mainly, not of habitual holiness, or the first habit of grace, but of actual holiness: whether internal in the exercise of grace, or external in the performance of duty. Thus holiness, I say, is necessary to salvation, as being the native necessary, and inseparable fruit of justification, or dying to the law; it is the justified man's way of living, or walking towards heaven. They that turn the grace of God into wantonness, they pervert the right end of grace, which teacheth us to deny ungodliness, and worldly lusts; and they that give up with the law as a rule of holiness, because they are, or think they are delivered from the law, as a covenant of works, they pervert the very end of that freedom, which is that they may live unto God; and no doubt, many among believers themselves are in danger of this sin: for I know no sin, but a believer is liable to it, if he be left to himself; and because many of them abuse grace, therefore God keeps the law spur at their side; for it is with many, as with dull lazy horses, so long as the spur is in their side, they ride quickly; but when that is removed, they become dull and heavy, and are ready to stand still: so, while the law exacted rigid obedience, and threatened damnation and hell, they were diligent, and durst not neglect a duty; they were tender in their walk: but now, being delivered from this spur, that was daily

pricking their sides, and seeing that Christ hath satisfied the law, which now can neither justify nor condemn them, they imagine they have no more to fear; and so they sin the more, and live securely, instead of living soberly, righteously, and godly. This is a turning the grace of God into wantonness, and a perverting of the very end of grace: and if any child of God here be guilty, remember that your heavenly Father will not let you pass unpunished; though he pardon your sins, yet he will take vengeance on your inventions. It is to prevent this wantonness in some, that the spur is kept long in their side; and they are kept many days and years, perhaps, under many legal shakings, fears, doubts, and tremblings, attaining to very little of any cheerful gospel-obedience; for the law cannot work that. And this leads me to another inference.

7. Hence, from this doctrine, we may see that the law can neither justify nor sanctify a sinner; it cannot justify him, for he must be dead to it in point of justification; it cannot sanctify him, for he never lives unto God, till he be dead to the law. On the one hand, "By the deeds of the law no flesh living can be justified:" why? Because you are dead in sin by nature, and can do nothing that the law requires, in the way that it requires it; and, though you would do anything, yet your doing is imperfect, but the law requires perfection; yea, though you could obey the law perfectly for the time to come, that will not make amends for former faults; there must be satisfaction; yea, suppose it were possible that you could do all this, and that, from your cradle to your grave, you never sinned; and were as free from original sin, and had as good a nature as ever Pelagius thought any had, and strength to keep the law, and did actually keep it perfectly, from your youth up; yet the law of works is broken in Adam, in him we all sinned, and that one sin is enough to damn the whole world, and would do so, if Christ did not redeem from the guilt thereof.—On the other hand, the law cannot sanctify any, it

works wrath; and, when the commandment comes, sin revives; it is the ministration of death every way, as I said before. But here a question may be moved, If the law can neither justify nor sanctify, what use is it for? We may answer, It is for many noble uses, both to the regenerate and unregenerate. To the unregenerate it is of use to conviction of sin; to break up the fallow-ground of the heart; to be a schoolmaster to lead to Christ, by convincing him of his absolute need of a Surety, and of his undone state without Christ.—And to the regenerate it is of use, to make them highly esteem Christ, whose righteousness answers the law in its commands and threatenings both; and it serves to give him a daily conviction of sin, that the man may more and more prize the pardon of sin, and seek daily unto the Lord, for pardoning and sanctifying grace; also, to let him see the intrinsic demerit of sin, while he sees hell threatened against it in that covenant; and thereupon may fear to offend that God who is a consuming fire, but rather that he may worship him with reverence and godly fear; not with a slavish fear, that he may be sent to hell, which is impossible; that is not his duty; he may have the overawing fear and apprehension of hell, but should not have a slavish tear of it; this fear of it he should not have, but the faith of it he ought to have, and many times need to have it, to terrify him from sin; which, from its own nature, leads to destruction; as a man that is bound, with a great chain, to a stake on the top of a high tower, though we cannot but know that, by reason of the chain, he is sure enough; yet, when he looks over the battlement, and sees the dreadful precipice, it scares him from going near the edge of the battlement. It is certain that believers, when they know not that they are under grace, may unwarrantably apply to themselves the sentence, of the law; unwarrantably, I say, because there is no condemnation to them that are in Christ, yet God may, for holy ends, suffer his conscience to be troubled with the fear of condemnation, that, being humbled, he may make the more use of Christ for righteousness and strength. In a word, the commands of the law, not formally, as a covenant; but materially, as a rule of life, serve to be an active directory for his walk; and, whoever walks according to this rule, peace be on them, and on all the Israel of God. Thus, it is of manifold use, though it can neither justify nor sanctify, which only the grace of the gospel can do.

8. Hence see what a mystery to the world religion is, and the difference betwixt God's judgment and man's; man thinks, to be dead to the law, is the way to live to sin; but God's word tells us, that to be dead to the law, is the way to live unto God. Why? here is a mystery, a holy riddle; and we are decrying holiness, when we preach in this apostolic strain? God forbid; nay, we declare unto you, in the name of God, that the way to be truly holy, is to quit with your false legal holiness the way to be truly righteous, is to quit your legal righteousness; yea, I tell you, man, that even in point of sanctification, "Except your righteousness exceed the righteousness of the Scribes and Pharisees, you shall not enter into the kingdom of God;" and you know they made long prayers, they fasted twice a-week, and gave alms of all that they possessed; and some of them were touching the law, blameless, and could say, "All these things have I done from my youth up;" and yet I say, Unless your holiness exceed their holiness, you shall never enter into the kingdom of God: and, till your unrighteous righteousness, and unholy holiness, be cried down in your heart, and the perfect righteousness of Christ cried up, true holiness you shall never have. Was Christ a friend to publicans or harlots? or, did he approve of their sins, when he said to these Pharisees, "Publicans and harlots go into the kingdom of God before you!" (Matt. 21:31). O beware of such blasphemous thoughts of a holy Jesus; nay, so far from that, that we may hence gather his abhorrence of their sins; only he would give us to know, that if sin keep them out of heaven, as much and more

will self-righteousness keep out the Pharisee, who must be rid of his righteousness, as well as his sins, before he get there.—O but religion is a mystery! to be dead to the law, in order to live unto God.

9. Hence we may see the miserable state of these that are alive, and the happy state of these that are dead to the law. Their state is miserable who are alive to the law; for, though they have a name to live, yet they are dead; legally dead, bound over to the wrath of God, and under the curse of the law: spiritually dead in sin, having no holiness, no godliness, acceptable to God through Jesus Christ. If they be any way awakened, and seeking life by the law, and the works thereof, what a madness is this, to seek the living among the dead? or to seek help where it cannot be had? God hath laid all our help upon Christ; and it is impossible to find justification or sanctification anywhere else. —But on the other hand, their state is happy who are dead to the law: for though they be dead, yet they live; they live a life of justification, and a life of sanctification thereupon; being dead to the law, they live unto God. O what a mercy it is, if God hath awakened your consciences, convinced you of sin and self-righteousness, and brought you off from the law! You see your extreme guilt, vileness, baseness, and wickedness; and it may be are groaning under the sense thereof: but God may have a glorious design in this, to bring you more and more off from the law, and from any confidence in the flesh, that you may build upon a better foundation, and be married to a better husband, even to Jesus Christ, that you may bring forth fruit unto God.

10.—Hence see the malignity of a legal spirit: if we must be dead to the law, that we may live unto God, then a legal spirit and temper must be a wicked and ungodly spirit: it is an ignorant spirit; if they were not ignorant of God's righteousness, they would never establish a righteousness of their own: but they are ignorant of the perfection of his law, the terror of his justice, the severity of his tribunal, and of their own natural weakness and wickedness, otherwise they would not dare to make anything a ground of their acceptance with God, except the blood and righteousness of his Son, It is a proud spirit, that will not let grace be exalted, but puts self, in the throne of Christ, and his righteousness. It is a filthy and abominable spirit and pollutes the man more and more: and God abhors it, as that which contradicts his most glorious plot. And it is a damning spirit, if it be not removed; "For the wicked shall be turned into hell:" and this man continues wicked still, even under the pretense of holiness; he is wicked and ungodly still, for he lives to himself, but not to God; for it is only these that are dead to the law, who live unto God.

CHAPTER 9

Of Examination

U se second, Of Examination. Try your state then, man, woman; you should try after, as well as before a communion: and there two things you should try here, 1. Whether you be dead to the law in point of justification? Whether you be living to the law, or living to God, in point of sanctification? Two as necessary points as are in all divinity, and such as are of the utmost concern in time, and through eternity.

First, Try whether you be dead to the law in point of justification. I might here give you marks of these that are alive to the law, and then marks of these that are dead to the law; but, seeing these will coincide, I join them together. I shall not multiply evidences, but you may try by these following: —

1. The man that is dead to the law hath got a sight of holiness in the glass of the law, and of his natural legal temper. Some think they have a good heart to God, and they can do so and so; but the believer dead to the law, he sees his heart, the worst piece in or about him; and that he cannot believe, he cannot repent, he cannot mortify sin; corruption is

like the giants of Anak. The man sees he is vile, with Job; "Behold, I am vile!" vile in every duty, in praying, communicating,

"Behold, I am vile!" He sees himself, and he sees his own legal temper. —The man that is alive to the law never sees his legal temper, nor his strong inclination to self-righteousness; the believer sees and finds something of this, even after he is made a gospel-saint; but the legalist never sees it. What, say they, would you have us Papists? Blessed be God, we are better instructed; we have no merit, our righteousness is rags! and yet, after all, there is a secret trusting in their own righteousness. Hath it ever been one exercise to you, how to get rid of your sins; and another, how to be rid of your righteousness?

2. The man that is dead to the law is tired and wearied out of it. Perhaps he hath been convinced of sin; and thereupon falling to the law, to this and the other duty; O! I deserve hell, for my sin is great; well, he endeavors to make amends, and to find peace, and so he runs to prayer and preaching thinking he will get peace, he repents, he resolves, and woe to the man that finds all his peace there without going further. But, behold, the man whom God shows mercy to, he goes on in these duties, but finds no peace, no rest, no satisfaction, he is tired out of it; his soul sinks with discouragement, and languishes and hangs down the head; and God thus unbottoms the man of himself.—Whereas, he that is alive to the law, he that takes up his rest and comfort in his duty: he hath the fear of wrath to come, and then he runs to his duty; the duty gives him ease, he is relieved, all is well; as a husband comforts his distressed wife, so obedience to the law comforts him, and the law heals him; it is the law that throws him down, and it is the law that raises him up again. But the man that is dead to the law, though the law terrify, yet it is not the law that satisfies him again.3. The man that is dead to the law, he knows what it is to act from Christ as his principle; and to him, as his end: he knows

what it is to perform duty from a borrowed strength. The legalist may, indeed speak soundly, and say, He can do nothing of himself without Christ; and yet he reads, prays, preaches, hears, communicates, and does all as if he had the power in his own hand. Let a man have never such an orthodox head, if he be not a believer in Christ, he is an Arminian and Pelagian all over; he knows not his own weakness; he looks not up for immediate influences.

And as self is his principle, so to self he acts as his end; as he that is joined to Christ brings forth children or fruit unto Christ; so he that is joined to the law: he does duty, it may, be, to hush the clamors of conscience, and give it ease; to keep himself out of hell, for he hath no will to be damned, and for the like ends. The believer being dead to the law, cannot perform duty, but by borrowed strength; he can do nothing till a gale of the Spirit come; he cannot bring forth children till the Spirit of God beget them in his soul: no, no; every, act of grace flows from a creating power; and, when he acts, the love of Christ especially, and the desire of communion and fellowship with God, constrains him; and the glory of God in Christ is his great end.

4. The believer, that is dead to the law, he hath vilifying thoughts of all he does: the Legalist over-values his duties: "Wherefore have we fasted, and thou hast not seen? Wherefore have we prayed, and thou hast not heard?" They challenge God as he were unjust, for not giving them what they merit: "God, I thank thee" said the Pharisee, "I am not as other men:" it was like a proud boasting of what he had done. But let the believer spend days and nights in prayer, and that with much liberty and enlargement, yet the issue of the work is, O my righteousness is filthy rags, a menstruous cloth! Woe to me, if I be not found in Christ, for my best duties deserve damnation; I find my praying, my worshipping, my communicating, full of atheism, unbelief, formality, and hypocrisy.

—The legalist over-rates his duties: he thinks more of what he hath done, than of what Christ hath done; and more of his praying on earth, than of Christ's pleading in heaven: he thinks more of his tears than of Christ's blood: he is proud of his humility, and never duly humbled.

5. The believer that is dead to the law, so far as he is dead thereto, his complaints and his comforts move in a gospel-channel. The legalist will complain more for want of holiness, than for want of Christ: seeing he hath taken up with a self-righteousness, it is his all, it is his happiness, it is his husband, it is his God; and when it is wanting, he cannot but be troubled. But the language of the man dead to the law is, O for Christ! O for a day of power! O to be wrapt up in the covenant of grace, to get an omnipotent power, determining me to comply with the gospel-offer! His comforts move in a gospel-channel. —But the legalist finds comfort in law-works, even in all his extremities in time: In the prospect of trouble, what comforts him?

Even this, that he hath done many good duties; he wraps up himself in a garment of his own weaving. Upon challenges of conscience, what comforts him, and gives him peace? He even covers himself with the same robe. In the prospect of judgment, what comforts him, and gives him peace? Why he hopes God will be merciful to him, because he hath a good profession, and said many good prayers, and done many good duties. But O sorry peacemaker. The only thing that gives a believer peace and ease, in these cases, is the law-biding righteousness of Christ, under which he desires to shroud himself: he flees to the blood of Christ, saying, O I am undone, unless my soul be wrapt up in the mantle of Christ's perfect righteousness; "I desire to be found in him:" upon this righteousness of Jesus do I venture my soul; I have no shift but this.—The legalist, I said, comforts himself in all his extremities with the law, till the extremity come, and then he finds himself cheated, miserably deceived; and hence,

O what a mercy is it, that the Lord drains a man of his legal comfort, that he may unhinge him off the law, and off his self-confidence! Oft-times, when God is bringing in his elect, he makes all the common work they had before to disappear. It may be, they had a profession, were morally serious, they had zeal, prayed with life, heard with affection; but behold now, all the streams of common influences are dried up; the poor soul finds he cannot pray, he cannot shed a tear, though he should be cast into hell: yea, he cannot think a right thought, though it should bring him to heaven; yea, he finds his heart hardened like a devil, and his mind bemisted with the darkness of hell.—Why? this is all in love, to induce him to relinquish himself, abandon the law as a covenant, and flee in unto and embrace the dear Son of God.6. The believer that is dead to the law is content to have his righteousness tried, and compared with the perfect law. As Christ is the Lord his righteousness, and this he knows is sufficient to answer all the demands and commands of the law, and he is not ashamed of this righteousness, but glories in it; so as to the works of holiness, whatever short-coming he is sensible of, yet he is content to be tried with the clearest light. Let omniscience descend, and make a critical search.

"Search me, O God, and see if there be any wicked way in me; and lead me in the way everlasting." I do not love to die with a lie in my right-hand: let all the inward corners of my heart be laid open before me: I am satisfied to know if I have a lawful husband, or not; if Christ be my husband, or not: he is content to be tried.—But the legalist, the man that is alive to the law, a searching sermon is uneasy to him; a gospel-sermon he cannot abide; a narrow trial he cannot endure; he thinks that the minister is too impartial to cast us all to hell; he hath stolen goods, and therefore dreads the light. Yea,

7. The man that is dead to the law, he hath got a soul-humbling sight, and saving view of the glory of Christ's righteousness, that made him quit with all his legal rags as loss and dung; even as the stars evanish out of sight when the sun arises. O hath Christ's glory, ever shined into your heart, man, woman, and made you see thousands of worlds to be nothing to him; thousands of righteousnesses of men and angels, to be nothing to his? Have you seen an utter impossibility of obtaining God's favor by any righteousness of yours? and such a sure ground of obtaining God's favor by any righteousness of yours? and such a sure ground of obtaining God's favor here, that your soul hath been made to renounce all other ways of repentance; and to see, admire, and rejoice in the glory of his way; and to approve it, as a device worthy of God, and suitable to you?

And have you found rest here? It is good. —The legalist is a stranger to such saving views of the glory of Christ, and his righteousness: having never got the Spirit of wisdom and revelation in the knowledge of Christ.

8. The man that is dead to the law, is in love with the doctrine of the gospel: "How beautiful upon the mountains, to them, are the feet of these that preach the glad tidings of peace!" Whereas he that is alive to the law, he always suspects the doctrine of the gospel, as if it were leading him away from the law, and away from holiness. Here is a mark that may well find out a Pharisaic generation; they suspect the doctrine of Christ, and his righteousness, as if it were a doctrine tending to licentiousness, and opposition to the law, a sign they never felt the power of the gospel upon their hearts, otherwise they would feel the revelation of the righteousness of Christ, from faith to faith, to be the power of God to their salvation; they would find, that never are they so much disposed to holy duties, as when they are under the influences of the Spirit of faith, discovering the glory of Christ, and his righteousness, to them. But an ignorant generation, that knows not the power and virtue of the gospel, still

suspects it as contrary to the law: this was the false charge against Christ of old, and against Stephen, (Acts 6:18), and against Paul, from which therefore he many times vindicates himself, (See Acts 18:13).

9. The man that is dead to the law, can, in some measure, put a difference betwixt Christ and a frame: whereas, he that is alive to the law, can never distinguish between Christ in duty, and a frame in duty? I suppose this is a hard question, how shall we know the difference betwixt Christ in duty, and a frame in duty? I will answer, in a word, The man that hath only a frame in duty, and not Christ in it, he is only pleased with his frame, his tears, his enlargements; he makes that his righteousness; he is content with that, and exalted with that; and now thinks all is well: but he that hath Christ in duty, and not a frame only, he is ready to cry, O I would have Christ! tears will not do the turn; my own heart hath deceived me a thousand times; I and my tears do not wash me, my frame does not sanctify me: this flowing of affection may be but a natural thing; it will not do; it is Christ I want: nothing but his blood can wash me: nothing but this blood can pacify his conscience; nothing but some views of Christ can give him solid quiet. A sweet frame may indeed be the chariot, in which Christ may ride towards the soul; but the gospel-believer is not so much taken up with the chariot, as with the glorious King who rides in it.

10. The man that is dead to the law, is dead to sin: sin hath not dominion over him, because he is not under the law, but under grace. The views of Christ are of a transforming nature; "Beholding his nature, we are changed." It is true, here the believer fears most of all, because of his shortcoming in point of sanctification and mortification of sin, because he finds iniquity prevailing against him; and how is it true that sin hath no dominion over him, he being not under the law, but under grace? Why, sin hath no righteous nor lawful dominion over believers;

the first husband is dead, and they, are married to Christ, the second husband; and therefore, they are not debtors to the flesh; though still the flesh craves them to obey it, yet it hath no just power so to do. Sin's just authority is exauthorated [deposed]; and Christ, by satisfying the law, which is the strength of sin, hath condemned sin in the flesh. Sin hath a sort of right to reign in wicked men, and these that are under the law; but none in the believer, who is delivered from the law, which is the strength of sin. Though it actually exercises authority, yet it is but an usurped authority; as sin hath no power nor authority to condemn the soul that is in Christ, so it hath no authority to reign; and sin shall never reign unto death over them, (Rom. 5:21). And the believer that hath cast off the authority to sin, as being no more his lawful king, may complain of its unjust oppression, and plead with a righteous God, that the power of sin may be more and more broken, and so it shall be. But the legalist, that is alive to the law, in regard that he is both under the commanding and condemning power of the law, he is under the commanding and condemning power of sin. The law commands him, and he obeys it as his lord; and sin commands him also, and he obeys it too, and makes his legal duties a plaster to cure his conscience of his sin: like Louis Xl. of France, who would swear a bloody oath, and, for a pardon, kiss a crucifix; and swear again, and then kiss it over again; and so, runs the round. However, the believer is delivered from the power of the law, and the power of sin too; having cast off the law as a covenant, and finding nothing to satisfy and still his conscience but the blood and righteousness of Christ, that satisfies divine justice; as in this way he finds rest from the curse of the law, so also some rest from the rule and dominion of sin; the faith of God's love in Christ does purify his heart, and kill his natural enmity, insomuch that he can attest, to his sweet experience, that the faith of the love of God in Christ is so far from leading him to licentiousness of life, or encouraging laziness, that he finds it the hottest fire in the world, to melt his heart for sin; and the strongest cord in the world, to bind him to duty, while the love of God is shed abroad upon him.—Try by these things, if you be dead to the law.—In a word, if you be dead to the law, then you will be living unto God; "I, through the law, am dead to the law, that I might live unto God." He is led sweetly to the law, as a rule of life. But here it may be inquired, how shall I know if I be living unto God? This leads me to the other part of the examination.

SECONDLY, Try if you be living unto God. Having enlarged so much upon the preceding head, and having offered several particulars upon this head already, in the doctrinal part, which may be improved by way of trial; therefore, I will offer you but these two marks of this.

1. If you be living unto God, then the Spirit of God will be the chief principle of your life; "The water that I shall give him, shall be in him a well of water, springing up to everlasting life," (John 4:14). The man hath not only the water within him, the graces of the Spirit; but the well itself, the Spirit himself dwelling in him. And as we know a springing-well, by seeing the water bullering and bubbling up; so a man may know he hath the Spirit, by the springing and flowing out of this water now and then. None have a life unto God, but these that have the Spirit of Christ in them, causing them to walk in his statutes; for, where the Spirit of life is, he is a Spirit of faith, and a Spirit of love; a Spirit of faith, leading men to the obedience of faith; which sets him to duty from the authority of God, and in dependence upon Christ, both as his strength for assistance, and as his righteousness for acceptance, in the performance thereof: a Spirit of love, leading the man to the obedience of love; and this obedience makes a man serve like a son, and not like a slave; and makes the service sweet and pleasant; "This is the love of God, that we keep his commandments; and his commandments are not grievous," (1 John 5:3).

This makes the believer's obedience, while he lives unto God, a mystery to the world, that reckon it a burden to keep the Sabbath, a burden to wait on ordinances, a burden to perform duties: why? on the other hand, when the believer is mounted up in the chariot of love, indeed it is a burden to him to leave off duty; it is a burden to him to leave ordinances; it is a burden to him to think of going back to the world again: Why? the matter is, he is about the, obedience of love, which makes the commands of God not grievous, but delicious. Try your obedience, and living to God, by this principle of it, the Spirit of God as a spirit of faith and love, leading to the obedience of faith and love.

2. If you be living unto God, then the glory of God will be the chief end of your life. But here a question may be propounded, how shall I know if the glory of God be the chief end in my obedience? Indeed, it is a material question. I will just offer a thought upon it. If the glory of God be the chief end of your life, then you will have a continual conflict with Self, and see how to get self-ends mortified. O! I see Self creeping in upon me, in all my preaching, praying, communicating; how shall I get this enemy killed? Here the flesh lusts against the Spirit, and the Spirit against the flesh, and these two are contrary the one to the other. The believer finds a war here against Self, as his greatest enemy; and it is his joy, and the triumph of his heart, when he gets Self dashed to the ground, and debased; when the loftiness thereof is brought down, and the Lord alone shall be exalted in him.—The man that hath God's glory in his chief end, he can sometimes trample even his own happiness under his feet, in a manner, when it comes in competition with the glory of God in Christ: the glory of God is of more worth than ten thousand heavens; and therefore the self-denied believer, before the divine glory should sink, would venture his all, though he had a thousand lives; "Blot me out of thy book," says Moses; "Let me be accursed," says Paul; and all was that God

might be glorified, that Christ might be magnified, and have a glorious name in the world. There were some things indeed extraordinary in that measure that Moses and Paul attained to; but there may be something like it, I think, though in a smaller measure, that believers way know in their experience: O! whatever should become of me, let thy name be glorified; let Christ have a numerous train to praise him to eternity; let me decrease, and let him increase; let him be exalted, though I should be forever abased; and, if it might contribute to his mounting of the throne, let me be even the footstool on which he may ascend.—The man prefers Christ's public interest before his own private interest; "If I forget thee, O Jerusalem, let my right hand forget her cunning. If I do not remember thee, let my tongue cleave to the roof of my mouth; if I do not prefer Jerusalem before my chief joy," (Ps. 137:5,6).In a word, the man that lives to God as his chief end, he acts in duties, because God is thereby honored and glorified; and he hates sin in himself and others, because God is thereby dishonored.

Finally, if you be living to God, your life, your obedience, will be influenced by the grace of the new covenant, being dead to the law, or to the old covenant: but of this I have spoken at large, on the fourth general head. —Thus much for the trial.

CHAPTER 10

Reproof of all Legalists, both doctrinal and practical

The Third Use may be for Lamentation over, together with Reproof of all Legalists, both doctrinal and practical.

1st, As to the doctrinal legalists, we might bewail and refute the legal schemes that take place in the world. I name these two.

1. The Popish scheme, denying the imputation of Christ's righteousness. The imputed righteousness of Christ is blasphemed by the Church of Rome; they call it an fictitious, imaginary air; a putative righteousness; contrary to the very strain of our Apostle in his epistle.

They talk of a twofold justification: their first justification is that, whereby an unjustified man becomes justified, or a wicked man becomes godly: where they confound justification and sanctification. The second is that, whereby a man already righteous becomes more and more righteous, more and more holy. We know no justification but one justification by faith, in the day of closing with Christ; laying hold on the blood of Christ, "Whom God hath set forth to be a propitiation, through faith, in his blood, to declare his righteousness for the remission of sins that are past, through the forbearance of God. To declare, I say, his righteousness, that he might be just, and the justifier of him which believeth in Jesus," (Rom. 3:25,26). It is a complete righteousness, we have it all at once; and it is not within us, but without us: it is in Christ inherently, but in us imputatively. They tell us that we are not justified by the works of the ceremonial law, but by the works of the moral law; they tell us that we are not justified by perfect obedience, but by imperfect; and, by an acceptilation, it is looked on by God as perfect; and, in a word, they acquaint us that we are justified, not meritoriously, and simply by works done in our own strength, but by works acted and done by the strength and assistance of the Spirit of God.—There is the Popish scheme.

2. The Baxterian scheme is also opposite to this gospel doctrine; they tell us that God hath made a new law with mankind, and obedience to that new law, and to its commands, is our righteousness: and obedience gives us a title to heaven, and gives us a title to Christ's blood, and to pardon; and the act of faith is our righteousness, not as it accepts of Christ's righteousness, but as it is an obedience to that new law; the very act and work of faith is, according to them, the righteousness itself; and this faith takes in all kind of works, namely, repentance, love, obedience, and ten or twelve duties of that sort; and all these together are our righteousness for justification. "Really," as one says upon this very head, "if the apostle Paul were alive, he would excommunicate such ministers."

2ndly, As to practical legalists; this generation is full of these. I know not a more reigning sin among professors: a gospel-strain is almost lost, and a gospel-method is almost forgotten. If we would go back to our reformers, we would see a gospel-spirit among them; but now the gospel-scheme is come under reproach, as if it were a new scheme; and some preach against it, write against it, reason against it, as if it were Antinomianism, and a going off from the law; as the Papists accused the

Protestants of old: why, what is the matter? A hellish, unholy, legal spirit reigns in the world. Now, in prosecuting of this Use, and that we may see how much ground there is to lament over, and bewail a legal temper that takes place, I would here, 1. Show some evidences of a legal spirit in the ungodly and unconverted. 2. Some evidences of a legal temper in believers themselves. 3. Show the cause of this legal temper that is in the world. 4. Show the evil and danger of it.

[1.] Some evidences of a legal temper, that is natural to the ungodly who, having no new nature, have no gospel-spirit at all. This may be evidenced in these four degrees of self, and legal pride.

1. While a man is just in the dead sleep of natural security, having no sight, nor sense of his sin, no conviction of, nor contrition for sin; even then, which is strange, he may imagine many times, that he is perfect, that he never breaks all the commandments of God, but keeps the whole law: the young Pharisee in the gospel is an eminent instance thereof; our Lord gives him an account of the commands of the law, and he had the insolent boldness to say to Christ, "All these things have I kept from my youth up;" and Paul, before his conversion, was stuffed with the same legal pride; "I was, touching the law, blameless." What means he by that? Why, it is as if he had said, I was such a staunch Pharisee, and religious zealot, that, as I never thought I broke any of the ten commandments, so I thought I had kept the whole law. Wonderful arrogance and ignorance, to imagine that a man in his fallen state can have a perfection and keep the whole law! And yet the elect of God, before their conversion, have found that they have been filled with such pride and insolent thoughts, as you see in Paul; yea, and many think little less; though they say they are sinners, yet they see not sin, and fancy they are conformable to the law: they have a good heart, they wrong no body, they are just in their

dealings, none can say, black is their eye; and here is their righteousness, being alive to the law.

2. Degree is, when men come to be convinced of sin and rebellion, and of their lost state, by reason of their having trampled the divine authority under foot, offended his Majesty, violated his law, provoked his anger; then, as if Christ were the most needless and useless thing in heaven or earth, they run to their repentance for an atonement, as Papists to their penances, and Pagans to their sacrifices, to atone their offended deities; as if there were no Day's-man, no Mediator betwixt God and man, to make atonement; Christ the Propitiation is altogether slighted; they hope to make atonement, and pacify God, by repenting seriously, and lamenting bitterly; and so they fall to work, praying, fasting, mourning, confessing with an absolute neglect of Christ; and, upon the back of all their legal fears, confessions and bitter lamentations, their awakened consciences are pleased and pacified. The storm that was raised there, is turned to a calm; a false peace takes place, not founded upon Christ, or his atoning blood, but upon their confessions, tears, prayers, whereby they think to disgorge and vomit up all the sins of their life, and to save themselves from them, and from the wrath that follows them. To this purpose was that saying of Augustine (it looks like a harsh saying, but had a good meaning,) namely, "That repentance damns more than sins do." When people are under any fearful apprehension of the wrath to come upon them for their sins, they flee to their repentance instead of fleeing to Christ, and that effectually destroys and ruins them.

3. Degree is when a man not only repents, but amends; he not only takes up resolutions of amendment of life, but actually studies obedience, reforms his way; he is at pains to get his life changed; but not to get his state changed: he is not taken up to get a new heart, but would have the old heart made a little better; he thinks a little mends will do

the business; and what is all this, but as one says, like the gilding of a rotten post; the post is rotten within, but it is finely gilded over without? It is but like the whitening of a sepulchre, that however white it may be without, yet it is full of dead men's bones within: it is like the painting of a chimney without, that is all black and sooty within; it is like adorning a dead corpse with sweet flowers. —The man is dead in sins and trespasses, notwithstanding all this.

4. Degree is beyond all this, gospel-light hath shined objectively upon them, and they are more illuminated than to be pleased with this: why? they hear of Christ, and that there is no salvation, no justification, without him; and therefore they act faith upon him in a legal way; they believe in him, not by a saving faith, but a temporary faith. As believers do perform gospel-obedience to the law, so unbelievers may have a legal faith of the gospel, a legal faith upon Christ; believing in their own strength; believing before ever he sees his inability to believe; before ever he sees his unwillingness to believe, before he be humbled under a sense of his absolute need of Christ; and before he sees what right and warrant he hath from the word. However, he fancies he hath closed with Christ, laid hold on his covenant; and this is the most subtle part of self-righteousness; yet, after all, he is the old man, still wedded to the law; and hence he hath no sanctification; no new nature, no new principle of spiritual life, no living unto God.

[2.] Some evidences of a legal temper that remains in believers themselves. 1. When their comfort is always up and down with their frame: if their frame be up, their comfort is up; if their frame be down, their comfort is down; if their frame be gone, their comfort is gone, their joy is withered; herein the legal spirit discovers itself. Whereas a gospel temper of soul would lead the man to rejoice, even when the changeable frame is gone, that the unchangeable covenant still remains; and to say, "Though the fig-tree should not blossom,—yet I will rejoice in the Lord." Though grace be at a low ebb with me, yet the ocean of grace is in Christ; and herein I rejoice though I find nothing but deadness in me, yet will I rejoice that there is life in him; though I be empty, yet will I rejoice that there is fulness in him; and this is to be communicated in his time and way.

2. It is a legal temper in the believer, when his assurance is lost by his challenges. It may be, the man attained some sweet measure of assurance, but behold sin prevails, conscience challenges him, and hereupon he razes all; this is an evidence of a legal temper, contrary to that gospel-spirit which we may see acting in David, "Iniquities prevail against me," (Ps. 65:3); it is against my heart, against my will, against my prayers, against my secret groans and wrestlings, against my resolutions, against my inclination they prevail: Shall I raze the foundation of my faith upon this account? No: I flee to the blood of the Lamb of God, for cleansing and purging both from the guilt and power of sin; and therefore, I will maintain my assurance and confidence in thee; "As for our transgressions, thou wilt purge them away."3. It is a legal temper, when faith is marred, either by sins or graces; I mean, either by the prevalence of sin, or the pride of grace. On the one hand, when the exercise of faith is marred by the prevalence of sin; when their known sense and feeling of out-breakings, either make a man stand a-back from Christ, or make him run away from him, by sinking discouragement or secret despair: this evidences much legality. Are you convinced of sin? Well then, you have the more need to come to Christ, and believe in him, and the less need to stay away from him. Peter had a prayer once, that looked like a set form of the devil's composing, "Lord, depart from me; for I am a sinful man." If it had run in a gospel-form, he would rather have said, "Lord, come to me; for I am a sinful man." Yet many believers have learned Peter's form of

prayer; Lord, I am such a sinful man, I dare not come to thee, nor believe that thou wilt come to me: Why? the more sinful thou art, the more need thou hast to come to him, and to employ him to come to you, and save you.—On the other hand, when the exercise of faith is marred by the pride of grace, this is a part of a legal temper; when believers trust more to their graces than to Christ, the fountain of all grace: when they look more to the strength of gracious habits, and trust more to them, than to the grace that is in Christ, in which they are called to be strong; "Be strong in the grace that is in Christ:" As by pouring of their sin, they are many times led off from depending on Christ, from constant incomes of actual influences. And hence, when a believer is lively, he is ready to think, he will never be dead again; when he is spiritual, that he will never be carnal again: when he is up in the mount, that he will never be down in the valley again, saying, "By thy favour my mountain stands strong;" he thinks it like mount Zion, that can never be shaken, and that he will never doubt again: but behold, "Thou didst hide thy face, and I was troubled:" my good frame was changed to a bad one: of a sudden my mount Zion was turned to a mount Sinai; all fears, all frowns, all darkness. Never hath a believer more need to act faith, and close dependence on the Lord, than when his graces and frames are most lively, lest self-confidence creep in, and he confides more in created grace, than in the fountain; out of whose fulness he is to have grace for grace. Let your frame be never so good, your faith never so strong, your grace never so lively, at any time, yet look up still for new influences; for, without momentary supplies and breathings from heaven, your gracious habits cannot act, and will not hold out a moment.

4. It is a legal temper, when peace is always marred by shortcomings; short-comings in the exercise of grace, short-comings in the mortifi-cation of sin, short-comings in holiness; when they pore upon these

short-comings, upon the weakness of grace on the one hand, and the strength of corruption on the other; upon such a sin and lusts that prevails, upon such a plague and distemper that affects them; insomuch that they cannot let in a word of comfort, they cannot hearken to the joyful sound of the gospel; like Israel, who harkened not to Moses, because of the anguish of their spirit: they look inward to themselves, and finding nothing there but failings, and infirmities, and plagues, instead of holiness, their peace is wholly demolished; because they do not, at the same time, look upward to Christ, to his blood and righteousness, and to his fulness; here is a legal temper.—So also, to the same purpose, when a man's peace and comfort rests only and always upon his sanctification, as if there were no other ground of joy, but a righteousness inherent: surely, when the joy of sanctification is greater than the joy of justification, it is an evidence of a legal temper; for the joy of justification is founded upon a law-bidding righteousness, the perfect obedience of the glorious Head, which is always the same unchangeable ground of joy to believers; whereas his sanctification is imperfect here, and cannot afford such peace and joy, as faith in a perfect obedience will give. The true circumcision rejoices in Christ, and in what they have in him, more than in what they have from him. But behold, even the believer is ready to be taken up with his sanctification, which is inherent, and so to be lifted up, when he attains to a good gale, a great measure of sanctification; corruption may abuse the privilege, and then he is proud and lifted up. It is true, communion with God, is of a humbling nature, and natively makes a man humble, and lively, and watchful; but when the good frame is wearing off, and corruption beginning to work again, if this nick of time be not noticed, and the believer on his guard, a proud thought may enter in, were it even upon a Paul wrapt up to the third heavens; "Lest I should be exalted above measure, a messenger of Satan was sent; a thorn in the flesh. O how does a legal temper run through every frame! When a man is dead and dull, then he is in danger of murmuring: and when he is active and lively, then he is in danger of swelling.

5. It is a legal temper, when a man's expectation of success, is built upon the minister that preaches: if the minister hath a weak gift, O they will not hear that man, at least they expect little good of him: if another hath great gifts, and a taking way, O now they expect heaven will come down: Why? this is an evidence of a legal temper: for a gospel temper will expect nothing, but in a gospel way; even by the powerful influences of the Spirit promised in the gospel. The gospel in any man's mouth is but a dead letter, without the Holy Ghost.

6. It is a legal temper, when the believer is under excessive discouragements, on whatever ground: it is an evidence he is too much under the law; for the law can give no encouragement, no settlement to the conscience; it is only Christ can give rest; "Come unto me, all ye that labour, and are heavy laden, and I will give you rest." What is it that discourages a believer when he is under this legal temper? Sometimes he is discouraged when he performs duty, and cannot find that presence, that sensible help he would have: why, then, he is quite dispirited.—Indeed he hath ground of mourning, when the Lord is away; he should be deeply humbled, for the causes of it: but when he is so dispirited, that he loses his confidence, and is beaten quite away from his faith and hope, questions his state, and gives way to slavish fear, that weakens his hands in duties, and draws his heart from duty, it is a token he is secretly hankering after the law; for the language of the heart of him is, O if I could pray with as much life, and hear with as much attention, and perform duty with as much vigor as I would be at! O then I would have a good hope; and so, it is not Christ, so much as the law, the old husband, that you desire to place your hope upon, while you are under that legal frame: the Apostle speaks of some

believers that desire to be under the law, (Gal. 4:21). Sometimes their discouragements arise from this, that they dare not apply the promises; and why so? because they think they are not for the like of them; such a promise belongs to such and such a good person; it is for a holy man, but not for the like of me: what is this but a legal temper, apprehending, that if you had such and such a legal righteousness, then God would be some way indebted to give you the promise! But O is not grace to be glorified in this new and gospel way! And therefore, the more of a gospel spirit you have, the more cheerfully will you embrace the promise, for this end, that having these promises, you may cleanse yourself, by sucking virtue from the breasts of the promise.

7. It is an evidence of a legal temper, when they are always straitened in duty. Sometimes they are discouraged, because they are so straitened in duty; and they are straitened in duty because they are so legal in it. Their discouragement flows from their straitening, and their straitening flows from their legal spirit; for a gospel spirit is a spirit of liberty. 1. When a believer is for ordinary straitened without life, without liberty, it is an evidence of a legal spirit; for, "Where the Spirit of the Lord is, there is liberty. The law of the spirit of life in Christ Jesus makes the man free from the law of sin and death," (Rom. 7:2). When one is influenced by the covenant of grace, he runs in the way of God's commandments. Though you have once known what it was to run sweetly in the Lord's way, yet if now you find a habitual indisposition to duties and religious exercises to be a heavy yoke, a grievous burden, this indisposition testifies against you, that though you have once known the gospel of Christ, yet now you are hankering after the, law. The Lord may indeed withdraw his presence from his people, for necessary ends, even from the man that hath much of the gospel-spirit; and such a man, amidst all his trials of that sort, will triumph in Christ, and say, "Though I have little in hand,

yet I have much in hope; whatever my own wants be, I have enough in Christ; however weak in myself, I am strong in him; imperfect in myself, but complete in him. But when, for ordinary, the person does not find pleasure in duty, hath little heart to it, and finds it not easy and light, but grievous, it is a token, that he is bearing the yoke of the law, or old covenant: For Christ's yoke is easy, and his burden is light; but this law yoke is heavy. The law, the first husband, requires hard, and heavy things, and does not help the sinner with strength; but Christ, the new husband, requires the same things, but he gives strength to perform; and what he requires of us, he works in us; "I can do all things, through Christ strengthening me:" were it to over-leap a wall, and fight armies of devils in my way.

It is a sign of a legal temper when a poor creature finds always discouragement, except when about religious duties; and finds no peace when about any other work, but is still racked, except when upon his knees, or going about some religious performance or other; it is a token of being knit and wedded too much to the first husband, for the law drives hard and craves hard, but Christ is very tender and gentle in his commands and demands; and a person under the influences of grace will find as much sweetness, even when eating and drinking, and when he is about his lawful employment sometimes, as when about religious exercises. Mistake me not here; think not that Christ will indulge his people in the omission of duty, that is not what I intend, God forbid; I know, and am persuaded that the sweetest hours the believer hath is when he enjoys communion with God in the ordinances and duties of his appointment: but yet, they that have much of a gospel-spirit can, with peace and freedom of mind, go about other things as the work of Christ; though it be a piece of self-denial to them not to be always with him, they would notwithstanding incline to be every minute with him, and are longing for uninterrupted communion and fellowship with him; yet the thing I say is, that their hearts are not disheartened, nor their spirit dispirited, when called to other things; and it savors much of a legal spirit when the poor exercised creatures can find no peace about their other lawful duties, unless they be still about duties that are properly religious duties, such as prayer, and reading, and hearing, and the like; for, in some sense, other duties, such as plowing, and sowing, and the like, may be turned to religious duties, by a spiritual-minded man, and such as have a gospel-spirit, while they carry a heavenly mind to their earthly work.

9. It is a sign of too much of a legal temper, when a man is not satisfied with the measure of grace that the Lord allows him, but frets against heaven because he hath not so much as others. Let none mistake me here either: no man ought, in any different way, to be content with any measure of grace; we are still to be going on to perfection, but, when we grudge and repine, and are pained at the heart, and murmur against God, because we have not this and that measure as others have, it is a symptom of hankering after the law. A gospel-spirit does not strive with God, but meekly waits upon the Sovereign, who will have mercy upon whom he will have mercy and dispenses freely of his gifts and graces as he pleaseth.

10. It is a sign of a legal temper when a person is more taken up with the gifts of Christ than with Christ himself; more taken up with any little thing they get from him than with himself. When they get any sensible grace, and sensible good affections, melting of heart, and melting of spirit; any inclination to what is good, any gifts or graces, whether more common or special, they admire these, and are not so much taken up with Christ himself. But the person that is evangelical in his actings, by what he gets, he is led to the giver; if this be sweet, O! He is infinitely sweeter that sent it: I embrace the token, and it draws out my heart the more after him, from whom it came.

11. It is a sign of being too much under the influence of the law, when the believer is possessed with a fretful spirit, and is not content with anything, for the gospel sweetens a man's frame of spirit. If the believer go to the law, he is constantly pained and wounded, and a diseased person is always a repining person, and this fretfulness is a sign that they are not sound at the bottom; but the gospel is health to the heart, and medicine to all the flesh. A gospel-spirit is a spirit of faith, a spirit of love, a spirit of power, and of a sound mind, (2 Tim. 1:7). And hence, take a believer, when he is much under the influence of the grace of the gospel, ten thousand little difficulties that sometimes fret him and put him out of humor will not move him then when he is living near Christ, and under the influence of the covenant of grace; but when, at other times, everything frets him, it is a sign that the law hath the ascendant, for "The law works wrath," (Rom. 4:15).

11. It is a sign of a legal spirit when, upon the back of religious duties, the man hath more freedom to sin; "Sin shall not have dominion over you; for you are not under the law, but under grace." The law irritates corruption, raises the devil, but cannot lay him; but the grace of God in Christ teaches to deny ungodliness and worldly, lusts. This grace only keeps down the devil, and lays him low, as it were; yea, bruises the serpent's head, and destroys the works of the devil.

When a man performs duty in a legal way, to quiet his conscience, why, then, when conscience is quieted with the duty, lust gets a vent like the whore of which we read, "I have offered my peace-offerings, this day have I paid my vows: come, let us take our fill of love," (Prov. 7:4).

But, when a man performs duty in a gospel-way, not merely to satisfy conscience, or pacify the judge, but to glorify God, to honor Christ, which is the great gospel end of performing duty; then this glory of God in Christ, that he hath in view, prompts him to desire, by the means of duty, to get the better of God's enemies in the heart; and, when he gets the victory, he desires to pursue his enemies, even to the death.

Now, my dear friends, if there be any believer here, I am sure some of these evidences, if not all, may find you out, to have too much of a legal temper about you. O, believers, you who have fled for refuge, to lay hold on the hope set before you, will you consider what danger you are in from Christ's rival, the law, as a covenant, your first husband, and how much you're following after that doth undo you? You, it may be, think you are in hazard from carnal friends, or from the world; but you cannot understand how you can be in hazard from the law: but you may be in the greatest hazard from that which you are least afraid of. Paul tells the believers here, and elsewhere, to whom he writes, what hazard they were in, even from those that pretended to preach the gospel, who were but ministers of the old covenant, who pressed, and knew nothing but to press the people to yield obedience and subjection to their old husband, the law; pretending to the greatest holiness and strictness of life; and pressing nothing but Do, do, and live. Nay, but says Paul, I, and all believers, have another way of living to God, and his glory, than by living on, or by the law, as a covenant; "I, through the law, am dead to the law, that I might live unto God." O, believer, arm yourself against all proxies that the law makes use of; study the nature, fulness, and freedom of the new covenant; and pray much for the spirit of wisdom and revelation in the knowledge of Christ, and his gospel. I go on to

CHAPTER 11

Causes of this legal temper

T he Third thing here proposed, which was to show the causes of this legal temper. Why is the world to set upon the law, as a covenant, and so little upon Christ, as the Lord their righteousness? I sum up all the reasons into this one, which I shall draw out into some particulars: and it is gross ignorance, proud ignorance; "For they being ignorant of God's righteousness, and going about to establish their own righteousness, have not submitted themselves unto the righteousness of God," (Rom. 10:3). The world is ignorant of God, ignorant of the law, ignorant of the gospel, ignorant of Christ, and his righteousness.

1. Ignorance of God is one cause of this legal temper. People are ignorant of the perfections of God; more particularly, they are ignorant of the holiness of God: if men saw what an infinite holy God he is, and what an infinite hatred he bears towards the least sin, or violation of his law; if they knew that a proud thought were enough to damn a million of angels, and that a wandering thought is enough to damn a million of worlds, would they entertain a fancy of being justified and accepted upon the ground of any legal righteousness of their own, whether natural or

gracious? Nay, they would not imagine to be thus accepted, if they did not think that God is such an one as themselves.—They are ignorant also of the justice of God, and the righteousness of that Judge, who will by no means clear the guilty; and if it were not so, that they were ignorant of his justice, would any guilty sinner hope to be cleared, and acquitted any other way, than upon the account of a ransom of infinite value? They are ignorant of the wisdom of God, in the glorious plan of redemption, and contrivance of salvation, by the righteousness of another, even of the God-man Christ Jesus. —Ignorance of these, and the like attributes and perfections of God, is the great cause of their being joined to the law, and alive to it.

2. Ignorance of the law is another cause of this legal temper and disposition; and here,

(1.) They are ignorant of the precept of the law in the extent, spirituality, holiness and perfection thereof: the young man in the gospel thought himself perfect; Why? he did not know the law. Paul thought himself blameless, when he was alive to the law; men think it a narrow rule, condemning only some gross enormities of life, and commanding only some outward materials of obedience; but they see not the commandment to be exceeding broad; hence they imagine, they can observe it perfectly well.

(2.) They are ignorant of the penalty of the law, the sanction of it: they do not believe that there is a curse entailed upon every disobedience; "Cursed is every one that continueth not in all things that are written in the book of the law to do them." Hence, they are foolishly fond of their own legal righteousness, not knowing the severity of the legal sanction.

(3.) They are ignorant of the end of the law, even of God's end and design in giving it. God gave the law to Israel with fire and thunder; For what end? Even to be a schoolmaster to lead them to Christ, (Gal.

3:24). "For Christ is the end of the law for righteousness, to everyone that believeth," (Rom. 10:4). But behold so ignorant was Israel of the end of the law, that, like the legal spirit in our own day, they thought it was given for this end, that they might obey it as a condition of life, as it bore the image and representation of a covenant of works; so they turned it directly to a covenant of works, saying, "All that the Lord hath commanded, we will do," (Ex. 19:8). If it had been possible or practicable, for them to have performed what they ignorantly promised, there would have been no need of Christ, or his righteousness either; "We Will Do," say they; there is obedience: yea, "We will do ALL that the LORD JEHOVAH hath commanded us:" there is exactly and perpetually perfect obedience; yea, WE will do all; WE ourselves; there is perfect personal obedience resolved upon: as if they had in their possession, all the power and holiness that Adam had in innocence.—What says Joshua to them, upon such a proud, ignorant and arrogant resolution as this? Indeed, he tells them, it was simply impossible for them; "Ye cannot serve the Lord, for he is a holy God," (Joshua 24:19). He is a holy God, and you are a sinful people; it is impossible for you to do what you say. The law was given them, to let them see their utter insufficiency and inability; to let them see their sins, and desert because of sin; that, under the fear of divine wrath, they might be obliged to have recourse to the Saviour. But they being ignorant of this great end of the law, set up an obedience of their own.

3. Ignorance of the gospel, is another cause of its legal temper; and here ignorance discovers itself in manifold instances.

(1.) They are ignorant of the promise of the gospel, such as that, "Surely shall one say, In the Lord have I righteousness and strength," (Isa. 45:24). Here is a sum of the gospel-promise; a promise of Christ, and of faith in him: "Surely shall one say;" here is a promise of faith, and faith working out from the heart to the mouth; for, "With the heart men believe unto righteousness, and with the mouth confession is made unto salvation." ONE shall say, what! no more but ONE? What a pity is it, that only one should say so? Indeed, it intimates, that very few shall be brought off from their legal temper: ONE shall say; not everyone; well but what will he say? "In the Lord have I righteousness and strength:" Righteousness, for justification; strength for sanctification: righteousness, to make me happy; strength to make me holy; righteousness, to give me a title to heaven; strength, to give me a meetness for heaven. I have all this, shall one say, by the appropriating act of faith; applying all to himself in particular, with assured confidence, according to the measure of faith: I have righteousness and strength: where hath he it? It is in the Lord I have it: I have it not in myself, nor in my own natural power; I have it not in my own free-will; I have it not in my walk and conversation; I have it not in my zeal or profession; I have it not in my religious duties or performances; I have it not in my heart or life: nay, certainly I have it not there; but, "Surely in the LORD have I righteousness and strength;" in the LORD only: men are ignorant of this.

(2) They are ignorant of the method of the gospel, in the application of grace promised, particularly in the command of believing, which belongs to the dispensation of the gospel; wherein the law, in its commands and threatenings both, is used in a subserviency to advance the ends of the gospel. Though the law doth not teach us to believe in Christ, yet he being revealed, it obliges us to believe in him; though the law reveals not a Saviour, yet the gospel revealing him, the law obliges us to come to him.—But now this method of the gospel, and dispensation thereof, is not known in the world; hence come legal undertakings of it; men confounding the command of believing, with the gospel to be believed: the duty of faith, with the object of faith; and so turn the gospel to a

new law, a new covenant of works; as if the act of believing were our righteousness for acceptance with God. Neither can they conceive the command of believing to be the great command, though God himself hath said, "This is his commandment, that ye believe in the name of his Son:" Nay, legalists cannot understand that; they think it is God's great command, that seeing they have sinned by breaking the law, they should repent by turning to it; seeing they have displeased God by their sins, they should please him by their repentance; seeing they have provoked him by their disobedience, they should pacify him with their obedience; seeing they have drawn down the curse by their transgressions, they should remove it by their reformation; They do not know that the great command is, To believe on the Son of God.

(3.) They are ignorant of the great end of the gospel, which is, to humble and abase the creature to the lowest, and to raise and exalt grace to the highest: that no flesh shall glory in God's presence, but that he that glorieth, shall glory in the Lord; "In the Lord shall all the seed of Israel be justified, and shall glory." That is the great end and design of the gospel: but the legal spirit is ignorant of that design.

(4.) They are ignorant of the gospel-covenant; the doctrinal and practical confounding of the two covenants of works and grace, is the great reason of this legal temper. And here people discover ignorance of the condition of the covenant; they are ignorant of the condition of the covenant of grace and works; the condition of the covenant of works, was personal obedience; the MAN himself that does these things shall live in them: and perfect obedience was required: a perfection of parts, a perfection of degrees, a perfection of duration. The condition of the covenant of grace is Christ's perfect obedience received by faith. There is much ignorance of this, at the root of all the legality that takes place in the world. They are ignorant of the form of the covenant: how by the covenant of works we get strength within ourselves, and by ourselves we could obey it; how, by the covenant of grace, our strength is without use as well as our righteousness; "In the Lord have I strength;" and we are to be strong in the Lord, not in ourselves, but in the Lord, and in the power of his might; to be strong in grace, not that grace that is in ourselves, but the grace that is in CHRIST JESUS.

4. Ignorance of Christ and his righteousness is a great cause of men's establishing a legal righteousness: "For they, being ignorant of God's righteousness, and going about to establish their own righteousness, have not submitted themselves unto the righteousness of God," (Ro m.10:3).—God was about to cast off a whole church, to reject them, and unchurch them: why? what is the reason? because they were such a proud pack, they would rather be damned with their own righteousness than saved by Christ's righteousness or obliged and beholden to him for it. They would not submit to it: why? because they are ignorant of it; they do not see the glory of it, as it is the righteousness of God; they do not see the necessity of it, because their own righteousness was reckoned sufficient; they do not see the fulness of it, as answering all the demands and commands of the law; they do not see the value of it, as sufficient to procure the favor of God, and purchase grace and glory; they do not see the acceptableness of it, as being the only righteousness with which God is well-pleased, and that thereby the law is magnified, and made honorable: they are ignorant of all this, and therefore they go about to establish a righteousness of their own, and will not submit to this. Their ignorance was a proud ignorance, and so it is with all by nature; we are filled with proud ignorance and ignorant pride, though our power be gone, our pride remains.

Chapter 12

The evil and danger of a legal temper

The Fourth thing here proposed was, The evil and danger of a legal temper, and legal obedience: why?

1. This legal way is a very unpleasant work, it is a wearisome work; "What a weariness is it," says the man. "He is wearied in the greatness of his way, and yet he says not, there is no hope," (Isa. 57:10).—It is true, the law hath sometimes its influences of comfort to its votaries, and stony ground hearers may receive the word with joy; and, no doubt, they may pray, and do other duties also with joy, but it is only a mood that soon vanishes, having no root in Christ. Can a dead man have pleasure in vital actions? Can a heavy stone incline upwards? O, but the legal soul is a miserable creature! The law drags him to duties, conscience presses him to work, saying, Fast, pray; pray, man; work for your life, repent, reform, as you would not be damned: but, behold, he cannot, though they be good duties he is called to; and the legal covenant, the legal minister, the legal conscience of him cries, Make brick, make brick, make brick: but, behold, he hath no straw, no straw, no straw, nothing to make it of. He

hath no strength, no grace, no communication; and so he tugs, he works, he sweats, but it is a heartless and unpleasant work.

2. Legal obedience is very unprofitable work, as well as unpleasant; "I will declare thy righteousness and thy work, for they shall not profit thee," (Isa. 27:12). The self-righteous Pharisee may fast twice a week, give alms of all that he hath; he may make long prayers, many prayers; he may both preach and pray frequently and fervently; yea, the poor legalist may work at his secret devotion and family devotion; he may wait on ordinances, and frequent communions, and run the whole round of duties; and, when he hath done this thirty, forty, fifty years, all the profit is, he gets hell for his pains; "To what purpose is the multitude of your sacrifices?" (Isa. 1: 2). All is unprofitable.

3. The legal obedience is very carnal, for it is a life wholly destitute of the Spirit: "This would I learn of you," says Paul, "if you would be doctors of the law, let me have a lesson from you, if you can give it; received ye the Spirit by the works of the law, or by the hearing of faith?" (Gal. 3:2). Was it by the works of the law? I suppose not: nay, the Spirit is not received in that way: it is in and by the gospel of Christ. The legalist is destitute of the Spirit; whatever fictitious holiness he may have, or real holiness he may pretend to, he wants a sanctifying work, sealing work: "Sensual, nor having the Spirit."

4. Legal obedience crosses the most glorious designs of heaven, particularly God's design in giving Christ, and Christ's design in coming to the world.

(1.) It crosses God's great design. What is that? It is even the exalting of his free grace: what is the great design of all the great works of God, viz., election, redemption, regeneration, providence? —Why does he choose one, and reject others? Why does he choose a wicked publican, and cast a righteous Pharisee to hell? Why does he redeem a poor, ignorant, ill-natured man or woman from their miserable state, and let the rich and learned go to hell? Why does he regenerate an elect soul after he hath been twenty, thirty years in the devil's service? And, after they are regenerate, why does he, in providence, let them fall into straits, wants, sins, manifold temptations, troubles, affliction, desertion, and heavy complaints on these accounts? Why? All is to exalt free grace in the issue. But now the legalist crosses this design of God; he would have self-exalted, his works exalted, instead of Christ, and free grace. He puts another righteousness in the room of the righteousness of Christ, and so takes the dung of his own righteousness, as Paul calls it, and casts it upon the face of free, rich, and sovereign grace, to cover, and hide, and darken it.—O, what a devilish design is this, in opposition to God's glorious design of making grace shine brightly!

(2.) It crosses Christ's great design in coming to the world the grand intention of the Son of God, in coming from heaven, was "To bring in an everlasting righteousness," (Dan. 9:24). But, behold, the legalist's design in establishing his own righteousness, is to make all Christ's labor to be lost labor; he endeavors to frustrate the very end of Christ's death, and makes it vain; "If righteousness come by the law, Christ is dead in vain," (Gal. 2:21). Instead of Christ's everlasting righteousness, he sets up a righteousness that cannot last half a day, nor half an hour; nay, not a moment.

5. Legal obedience hath the evil of blasphemy in it. It reproaches the righteousness of Christ, as if it were not sufficient, as if his atonement were not perfect, as if his satisfaction were not full, as if his obedience were not perfect, unless it be patched up with the rags of the man's own righteousness. Is not Christ's righteousness perfect without their addition? O, do not blaspheme the Son of God, and say in effect, his

obedience was not a divine, perfect obedience, for thus you reproach his fulness and sufficiency.

6. Legal obedience issues in a terrible disappointment; the poor deluded man thinks, his prayers and duties, that he hath been performing for so many years, will make an excellent robe to cover him; I hope, says the man, I have something that will contribute to make me die in peace; I have something to make me stand in judgment, that others have not; for many a duty have I performed, many a prayer have I made, these twenty or thirty years; and many times have I prayed with very much warmness of affection, and liveliness of frame, and therefore I have a good hope, that God will be pleased, and all will be well with me. But O what a fearful disappointment does the man meet with! Death comes; and if he die in the same legal dream, he goes down to the grave with a lie in his right hand; "The hypocrite's hope is like the spider's web;" Why! What comes of it? The spider works it out of her own bowels: it is her house, it is her food, it is her fence; there she dwells, there she feeds, there she secures and shelters herself for a while; but at the close of the day, or the end of the week, the besom [a broom of twigs] comes along, and sweeps her and her lodging, and all to the ground. Even so, the legalist, he works a web out of his own bowels, he wraps himself in this garment of his own spinning; here he dwells, here he works, here he feeds, here he shelters himself from all challenges, and apprehensions of danger; but behold the besom of death and destruction comes, and sweeps him, and his refuge of lies down to the bottomless pit. If his eyes be open on a death-bed to see hell, to see the justice of God, to see the spirituality of the law, the imperfection of his duties, the emptiness of his performances, and the sandy foundation he hath been building his faith upon, then his conscience roars, his heart despairs: he hath no peace, no comfort; but finds himself miserably disappointed. If his eyes be not open: what then?

why, he dies in a delusion, as he lived, sinks into the lake of fire; and in hell he opens his eyes, and finds himself eternally disappointed.—O see then, what ground there is to lament over this legal temper, which is indeed a damnable temper, where it hath a full reign.

Use Fourth, viz.—Of Exhortation, both to them that are alive to the law, and to them that are dead to the law, of whom the text especially speaks.

1st, To unbelievers, and all these that are alive to the law. O! for the Lord's sake, take no rest till you get out of that damnable state! O consider what you are doing, so long as you are not dead to the law; the best thing that you are doing, in that case is, that you are building your residence about the old rotten walls of the covenant of works. Perhaps you think you are a good Protestant, you are a good Christian, you have a good heart, you perform good duties, you have partaken of good ordinances, and what evil should you fear?

1. I assure you, that you are under the curse of the law of works; "Cursed is everyone that continueth not in all things that are written in the book of the law, to do them." And while you are under the law, and seeking to establish a law righteousness of your own, all the people of God are obliged to say, that God is in the right to curse you; they are obliged to say Amen, to all the curses of the Bible against you; Cursed is he that confirmeth not all the words of this law; and all the people shall say, AMEN," (Deut. 27:26). If you will take the old covenant of doing for life, and justification, then you must take it with a vengeance, unless you do perfectly, and do to purpose, which is impossible for you: "Cursed is every one that continueth not in all things that are written in the book of the law, to do them:" And all believers can say AMEN to it, in the words of Paul; "Let him that loves not our Lord Jesus Christ, be ANATHEMA MARANATHA," [i.e. accursed until the Lord come,]

(1 Cor. 16:22). While you are under the law, no blessing belongs to you, but all divine curses; if you will not get out of your legal righteousness, and get under the gospel covert of the blood of Jesus, nothing but terror belongs to you; and nothing but terrors and curses can I preach to you: for, "As many as are of the works of the law, are under the curse."

2. I must tell you, as you are under the curse of the law, so you are under the command of the law; Do and Live. Though by the gospel-call, you are not obliged indeed to seek righteousness in yourself, in order to life, but to seek it in Christ; yet by your unbelief, you keep yourself under the command of the law; "if thou wilt enter into life, keep the commandment;" keep it perfectly, or else vengeance shall overtake you. It is not your little endeavors that will satisfy the law; though you should read, fast, mourn, and shed tears of blood all your days, it will not avail, or be to any purpose, in satisfying the law's demands: if you will pay any duty to the law, as a covenant, you are a debtor to fulfill the WHOLE law, (Gal. 5:3). The law is a chain that is linked together, and if you take one link off it, the weight of the whole chain will be upon you; and so, if you will do anything in obedience to the law, that you may be thereby saved and justified, you are under bondage to the whole law; and bound to do everything perfectly that you may be justified. O the miserable bondage that you are under! You will never be able to satisfy the law; and so you are condemned already; yea, let me tell you more, you area wicked, ungodly creature; whatever you seem to be to others, or think you are yourself; yet, being alive to the law, you are a stranger to the life of God; for, till you be dead to the law, you shall never live unto God: though you look like an angel of light for holiness, yet, being alive to the law, you have no true holiness nor godliness. Ye that are still leaning to your works, then you will meet with a sad disappointment; for, "By the deeds of the law, no flesh living can be justified."—But there are others, who seem

to be upon another extreme; they say, the law is now abrogated, and we are not to seek justification or salvation that way; and therefore we are careless about the law, or about any duty of obedience.—Yea, but let me tell you your doom out of the law also; you are a desperate sinner: because you cannot satisfy the curse of the law, therefore you run away from the commands of the law, and run away to the devil, instead of running to Christ.

But I will tell you, though the law cannot justify, or save you, yet it can condemn you: it hath power to condemn you, though it hath none to save you; and it will condemn, and does condemn you, and all that are out of Christ; and therefore, for every sin that you are guilty of, you must answer; and every sin is enough to damn you, by virtue of the law. O then, may this be a mean to move you all that are under the law, to seek in to Christ, who is the end of the law for righteousness, to everyone that believeth! Come, poor, cursed, condemned, ungodly sinner, if you would live unto God here, and live with him hereafter, come out from under the heavy yoke of the law: Christ hath a good and perfect law-biding righteousness to give you; though you have nothing to bring to him, but sin, and guilt, and misery, and hell about you, yet come to him; and if you cannot come, O go to him, and tell him that you cannot come; and plead, that, by his omnipotent power, he may draw you; and if you do so in truth, it is one to a thousand, if he does not meet you half-way. O man, you cannot be saved, to the credit of God's holiness, unless you join with Christ's righteousness, which answers also the threatening of the law, and satisfies the justice of God. In this way, mercy can take vent, to the credit and honor of all God's perfections. O man, woman, are you for this way of it? O then say, Farewell to the law of works forever; here is a more noble and glorious way. O blessed be God forever, if that be the bargain betwixt Christ's righteousness and

your soul! O may the Lord draw you to it! But now, 2dly. To you that
are believers, and have closed with Christ, and so are dead to the law:
Remember, you are not to live a lawless life for all that. My exhortation
to you is, that, being dead to the law, you live unto God. Let me offer
some motives and directions, and the rather that I have taken some pains
to gather together and lay before you many things relative to a legal
temper, for guarding you against the Neonomian extreme, on the one
hand, let men beware lest your carnal hearts abuse this doctrine of grace
to Antinomian licentiousness, on the other hand.

Sure I am, the gospel-doctrine of itself hath no such tendency: though
an ignorant world may suspect the doctrine of the gospel, the doctrine
of Christ's righteousness, as if it were against a personal righteousness, or
holiness; I declare to you, in the name of JEHOVAH, that the contrary
is true; and assure you, that you will never live according to the law, as a
rule of holiness, till you be dead to the law, as a covenant and condition
of life: "He that hath ears to hear, let him hear."

If the light of the glorious gospel, even the light of the glory of God, in
the face of Jesus Christ, did once shine into your hearts, then, beholding
this glory of the Lord, you would be changed into the same image, from
glory to glory, by the Spirit of the Lord; yea, to believe the gospel savingly,
is the way to fulfill perfectly. The true believer may be said to fulfill the
law, both as it is a covenant, and as it is a rule: As it is a covenant, he
fulfils it perfectly and legally in his Head and Surety, in whom he hath
perfect, everlasting righteousness: And as it is a rule, he fulfils it perfectly
also, with a perfection of parts here, and a perfection of degrees hereafter:
and in both these respects may that word be explained, (Rom. 1:3,4),
where the righteousness of the law is said to be fulfilled in believers,
whose character is, That they walk not after the flesh, but after the Spirit.
Now, I would press you to this spiritual walk, this holy life, which is

a living unto God; for, though your holiness be not necessary for your justification, that is the damnable doctrine of Popery; though, I say, it be not necessary for your justification, because you are dead to the law, in point of justification; yet it is necessary, because you are dead to the law, for this very, end, that you may live unto God, in point of sanctification, and that you may be holy. More particularly for motives, consider the necessity of holiness, in these following particulars.

1. It is necessary in respect of God; and here (to use the method of a great divine on this head) consider how the will of God, the love of God, the glory of God, obliges you in particular, believer, to live unto God.

(1.) The sovereign will of God obliges you to holiness; "This is the will of God, even your sanctification," (1 Thess. 4:3). It is the will of God the Father, he hath ordained it: "We are his workmanship, created in Christ Jesus unto good works, which God before ordained that we should walk therein.""—It is the will of God the Son; "I have ordained you that you should bring forth fruit, and that it should remain," (John 15:16). It is the will of God the Holy Ghost, whom we grieve by our sins, if we do not study holiness.

(2.) The love of God obliges you to holiness; yea, this is the end of the electing love of the Father, the purchasing love of the Son, and the operating love of the Holy Ghost. It is the peculiar end of the electing love of the Father, who hath chosen us, that we should be holy, and unblameable before him in love, "He hath chosen us to salvation, through sanctification of the Spirit," (Eph. 1:4).—It is the peculiar end of the purchasing love of the Son, "Who gave himself for us, that he might redeem us from all iniquity, and purify to himself a peculiar people, zealous of good works," (Titus 2:14). And who loved his church, and gave himself for it that he might sanctify and cleanse it by the washing of water, and present it to himself a glorious church, not having spot, nor wrinkle, nor any such thing, but that it should be holy, and without blemish," (Eph. 5:25-27).—It is also the peculiar end of the operating love of the Holy Ghost; his whole work in us, and for us, consisting in preparing us for, and enabling us to the duties of holiness, and bringing forth the fruit thereof in us.—Believer, if you have any regard to the sovereignty of God, Father, Son, and Holy Ghost; any regard to the love of God, Father, Son, and Holy Ghost, it obliges you to holiness of heart and life.

(3.) The glory of God obliges you to holiness and makes it necessary. Would you glorify the Father? Then, "Let your light so shine before men, that they seeing your good works, may glorify God. Herein is my Father glorified, that ye bear much fruit."—Would you glorify the Son? "It is the will of God, that all men honor the Son, even as they, honor the Father." And how is this done? Even by believing in him and obeying him: "Ye are my friends [ye, evidence yourselves to be so], if ye do whatsoever I command you." Would you glorify the Holy Ghost? It is by studying holiness; for we are his temple; and holiness becomes his house and temple forever; and he is dishonored, when his temple is defiled. Surely, believer, when I speak to you, I cannot be supposed to speak to one, that neither regards the sovereign will, love, nor glory of God, Father, Son, and Holy Ghost; though your holiness should all be lost, and never regarded, which is impossible; yet here is reason enough for it.

2. Holiness is necessary in respect of yourselves; you are necessarily obliged to holiness; your own honor and peace is concerned here: It is gainful; "Godliness is great gain, having the promise of this life, and that which is to come." It is pleasant; for, "Wisdom's ways are pleasantness, and all her paths are peace. There is no peace, saith my God, to the wicked; but the fruit of righteousness is peace, and the effect of righteousness, quietness and assurance forever."

Yea, it is honorable, and the greatest honor you can be advanced unto; to be holy, is to be like unto God.

3. Holiness is necessary in respect of others; you are obliged to holiness: it may tend to the conviction and conversion of others. On the one hand, it may tend to their conviction, and to stop their mouths, who are enemies of God, and that both here and hereafter.

(1.) It may stop their mouths here in a present world, as you see, "This is the will of God, that with well-doing, you may put to silence the ignorance of foolish men," (1 Pet. 2:15). Ignorant fools may call you hypocrites; they may call you Antinomians, and enemies to the law: now, by well-doing, you give them an unanswerable document, that though you be dead to the law, as a covenant, yet you put honor upon the law, as a rule of holiness: and so make them ashamed of their base calumny, according to that, "Having a good conscience, that whereas they speak evil of you, as of evil-doers, they may be ashamed that falsely accuse your good conversation in Christ," (2 Pet. 3:16). And,

(2.) Holiness in you, believer, may tend to stop the mouths of God's enemies hereafter, in the day of judgment: it is said, "The saints shall judge the world," not only as they will be assessors with the Son of God, and applaud him in all his judicial proceedings: but in regard their holiness and good works will tend to the confusion and conviction of the wicked. And indeed, the good works of the saints will meet them one day, with a changed countenance, that they shall scarce know them; they see them now to be all black, defiled, and deformed; but they will then be brought forth beautiful and glorious, to the shame of the wicked, (Matt. 25:34-40). On the other hand, your holiness may tend to the conversion of others; "Having your conversation honest among the Gentiles, that whereas they speak against you as evil doers, they may, by your good works which they shall behold, glorify God in the day of visitation,"

(1 Pet. 2:12). The holiness of professors hath sometimes tended to the conversion of the profane, who, when the day of their gracious visitation hath come, have glorified God on that account, (1 Pet. 3:1,2); and therefore, says Paul, "This is a faithful saying, and these things I will, that thou affirm constantly, that they which have believed in God, be careful to maintain good works: for these things are good and profitable unto men," (Tit. 3:18).

4. Holiness is necessary, in respect of your state; you stand obliged to holiness. Are you in a justified state, accepted into friendship with a holy God, who is of purer eyes than to behold iniquity? Should you not evidence your justification by your sanctification? Is it not necessary that you should be holy, if you dwell in the presence, walk in the sight, and lie in the bosom of such a holy God? Are you in a sanctified state? Wherefore was you regenerate? Wherefore got you a new heart, and a new nature, and a holy principle of grace, but that you should be holy?—Are

you in an adopted state? Why so? but that you should live like the children of God, and be followers of God, as dear children? O! was you not justified, adopted, and sanctified for this end, that you might live unto God? If we be believers, what a shame is it for us, to live unsuitably to our state, as many times we do? Is that all the thanks we give to God for his favors, that we should trample his statutes under our feet, dishonor his name, break his laws, and grieve his Spirit"? It does not become you; it is not like you, believer: he hath loved you with an everlasting love, and drawn you with loving kindness: will you act like a devil, in enmity against him, because he acted like a God of love towards you? O fie for shame, believer! "Tell it not in Gath, publish it not in the streets of Askelon; lest the daughters of the Philistines rejoice, lest the daughters of the uncircumcised triumph," (2 Sam. 1:20). Have we not the hope of glory? And shall we not, having this hope, purify ourselves even as he is pure? —Are we partakers of the precious promises? Then, "Having these promises, dearly beloved, let us cleanse ourselves from all filthiness of the flesh and spirit, and perfect holiness in the fear of the Lord."—Are we heirs of glory? And shall we not seek to have our right and title unto glory cleared? "Blessed are they that do his commandments, that they may have right to the tree of life, and may enter in through the gates to the city," (Rev. 22:14): That is, either that your right may be, made evident, according to that word, "Ye are my friends, if you do whatsoever I command you:" That is, you thus evidence yourselves to be my friends; or concerning this right, know that there is a right of merit, and a right of meetness, both necessary: a right of merit, believer, you have not in yourself, but in Christ; and that is established in justification, through the righteousness of Christ: a right of meetness you must have in yourself from Christ, and that is in sanctification and holiness.—What shall I say? Are you not dead to the law, that you may live unto God? Are you not to testify your gratitude towards him that hath provided another law-righteousness than your own? Are you not to difference yourself from the world, that are walking in the broad way to hell and damnation, and under the curse of the law, and the wrath of God? Are you not delivered from the wrath to come, and of all men in the world under the greatest obligations to be holy?

Should you not study to please that God that hath pitied you? Hath he washed you in his blood?

And ought you not, through his grace to study to let it be known to the world, that his blood hath a virtue to sanctify you? —Yea, hath he not promised, "Sin shall not have dominion over you, because ye are not under the law, but under grace?" Should ye not study through his grace, to let it be seen, that his promise is verified in you?

5. Holiness is necessary in respect of the danger you are in, if you do not study holiness. If you be a child of God, you are indeed freed from the curse of the covenant of works, that penalty can never reach you; but, is it nothing to you, that your heavenly Father should chastise you, hide his face from you, deny an answer to your prayers, hide your evidences of heaven from you, give you up to the tyranny of your lusts, and then take vengeance on your inventions.

6. Holiness is necessary in respect of the advantage herein. You are obliged to holiness; why? in this way you may come to live joyfully, and die comfortably: in this way your integrity may be supported, as it was with Job; in this way you may come to have sweet communion with God, according to Christ's promise, "He that hath my commandments and keepeth them, he it is that loves me;—and I will love him, and will manifest myself to him," (John 14:21). In this way you shall be fitted for serving him in your generation, (2 Tim. 2:19). In this way you will have an evidence of your justification, (1 John 3:9). In this way you shall bring down the blessing of God on every work of your hand, all that ye shall do shall prosper, (Ps. 1:4). Yea, in this way you shall become a public good, a common good, a blessing, and a benefit to all about you, both in communicating good to them with whom you converse, and in diverting judgments from these that are about you, as ten righteous men would have preserved Sodom: O what a Sodom is the present generation! And as it is like Sodom and Gomorrah, and perhaps a thousand times worse, in respect of sins against law and gospel light, which Sodom never had; so, if the Lord do not leave us a remnant, we shall be like Sodom and Gomorrah, in respect of judgments.—All these things, and a thousand more that might be adduced, should press you mightily to the study of holiness, and living unto God: you are dead to the law, that you may live unto God. But next, For Direction. Now, here the question may be

propounded, O, how shall I live unto God? I shall offer you no directions but one, which my text leads me to, and it is this. If you would live unto God, O study to be more and more dead to the law. The more you are dead to the law as a covenant, the more will you live according to the law as a rule: what! do you not find a legal spirit that remains with you, and weakens your hand in duties of holiness? When you are wrestling at duties in your own natural strength, it is a legal, old covenant way: and do you not find it a hard, heavy, wearisome task? I suppose there is little holiness there; but, when you are leaning on the strength of Christ, do you not find your soul enlarged and quickened in duty?

When you perform duty from a principle of slavish fear, that is a legal way; and, do you not find your hearts weakened, and little heart to the work?—But, on the contrary, when the love of Christ constrains you, is it not then that you run with pleasure in the ways of his commandments? Yea, sin hath dominion over you when you are, and in so far as you are under the law, for the motions of sin are by the law; the law irritates corruption, and cannot subdue it, for it is the grace of God revealed in the gospel that effectually teaches to deny ungodliness and worldly lusts. To be dead to the law is to be married to Christ, it is to be brought off from the first Adam and united to the second Adam. And, believer, as you are in Christ, so you are to abide in him, if you would be fruitful, and live unto God; "As the branch cannot bear fruit of itself, except it abide in the vine: no more can ye, except ye abide in me," (John 15:4). Now, to abide in him is just to be strong in the grace that is in him, and to continue to be strong in him by faith, and this is necessary in order to fruitfulness; as, though an imp be grafted into the root, if it be not fastened and take firm rooting, it does not come to fruitfulness; so the sinner is made a Christian by being cut off from the law, and engrafted into Christ; but he is not a fruitful Christian if he do not take a strong

grip of Christ, and draw virtue from him; therefore, "Abide in me, and I
in you," says Christ, and O! but it is well said, for, if he do not abide in us,
we cannot abide in him. We will never abide in him by the grace of faith,
unless he abide in us by the Spirit of faith. If we provoke God to take
away his Spirit, our faith fades, fails, and decays, and then we depart from
the Lord by an evil heart of unbelief.—Here is the way, then, to live unto
God, and to bring forth fruit to him; even to die more and more to the
first husband, the law, and to live by faith upon your blessed Husband,
Christ.

Question: But, by what outward means should we thus live? May we
not neglect duties, since we are dead to the law? Nay, God forbid. It
was the devil's temptation to Christ, to cast himself headlong from the
temple, because God had promised to preserve him in all his ways; so,
believer, God hath promised to preserve you; he hath promised that sin
shall not have dominion over you; and that you shall never perish; and
is the devil tempting you, therefore, to throw yourself down headlong
from the temple, and from temple-means and ordinances, public and
private? O, tell that abominable devil, as Christ did, "It is written, Thou
shalt not tempt the Lord thy God." If you neglect means you tempt the
Lord your God, who hath commanded you to use means, and made
this the method of the communication of grace and strength, to wit,
in the use of such means as faith, prayer, reading, hearing, meditation,
watchfulness; therefore, O be diligent in the use of these means: only,
do not confide in the means, by putting them in Christ's room; give
means their own room, and do not expect, without the grace of the
new covenant, that means will do the business. Grace is the spring from
which the living water does flow, and means are the channel and pipes
through which the water is conveyed; and if the fountain do not send out
streams, all the conduits and pipes in the world can never convey it unto

us. Therefore, in the use of means, be still looking to the Lord; look to him, both for grace to use the means, and for grace to bless the means. If you lay any stress upon the means, they become unprofitable. In the use of these means, O cry, cry mightily to the Lord, that he would kill your self-confidence: cry for the Spirit of life, to quicken you, that you may live unto God; for, till the Spirit of life enter into the dry bones, there will be no stirring, no motion, no living to God: cry for the Spirit of faith, so as you may say, with Paul, in the context, "I live, yet not I, but Christ liveth in me; and the life I live is by the faith of the Son of God, who loved me, and gave himself for me." O, cry for faith, and the assurance of faith: no doubt, one may have faith, and yet want that assurance which we commonly call so; but, whether there be some kind of assurance or persuasion in the nature of faith, is a question that I do not here enter upon: only, this I am sure of, from the word of God, that doubting is no part of faith, for faith and doubting are as opposite as light and darkness. Some believers, indeed, have many doubts: why? because they have little faith, little faith, little faith: "O, thou of little faith, wherefore didst thou doubt?" And I find the believer who walks in darkness, and hath no light, he is directed to faith, as the antidote against his darkness and doubting; "Let him trust in the name of the Lord, and stay himself upon his God." Cry, I say, for the Spirit, and faith will work by love: cry for a gospel-spirit; for I testify, in the Lord's name, that gospel-holiness will never flourish among us, or in the generation, till we be more free of a legal spirit; and that we will not live unto God unless we be dead to the law.